D0341933

# The **Complete** Book of **Quilting**

# The Complete
# Book of Quilting
## The
## Book of

## Maggi McCormick Gordon

**kp books**
*An Imprint of F+W Publications*

700 East State Street • Iola, WI 54990-0001
715-445-2214 • 888-457-2873

Published by KP Books
700 East State Street, Iola WI 54990-0001

1  3  5  7  9  8  6  4  2

Library of Congress Cataloguing-in-Publication
Data: 2005929003

ISBN: 0873499557

Designed by Liz Sephton
Indexed by Wordwork
Photography Mark Hines

Reproduction by Classicscan Pte Ltd, Singapore
Printed and bound by Imago, Thailand

# Contents

# How this book works

This book was planned and designed to give quiltmakers a good grounding in a number of the most popular and widely used techniques for creating a quilt. Whether you are a beginner who is just learning, a learner who is eager to expand skills, or a more experienced quilter looking for new ideas, you'll find something to inspire you in these pages.

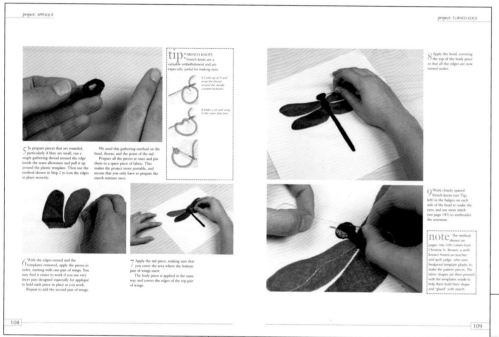

**TECHNIQUES**

*All the basic techniques you need to make a quilt, from piecing and applying to quilting and binding, are included as step-by-step instructions in Chapter 2.*

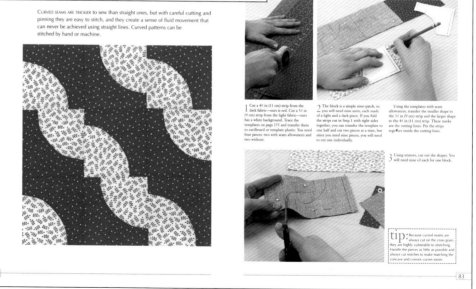

**PROJECT INSTRUCTIONS**

*Chapters 3 (Patchwork) 4 (Appliqué) and 5 (Quilting) contain specific projects assembled following instructions detailing the steps required to finish a block, as here, or a small project. Many contain Tips or Notes to provide extra information relevant to the project or the technique used.*

## PROJECT QUILTS

*A number of the project blocks were designed to work together to make quilts to demonstrate various aspects of finishing a quilt, discussed in some detail on page 60.*

*The smaller piece on the left is a sampler of three different red, white, and blue blocks and shows sashing with corner blocks (pages 58–59), plain borders and borders with corner squares (pages 58–61), and setting a quilt "on point" (page 60).*

*The larger piece (below), entitled "Taking Flight" and made from various appliquéd and quilted blocks from Chapters 4 and 5, is sashed (page 58), bordered (page 59), and set square (page 60).*

# Introduction

Calling any book "complete" is of course an exaggeration. Such a book about quilting, as with most subjects, would be too heavy to lift. But my intention in writing this "complete" book is to offer to beginner and intermediate quilters a wealth of information about the subject—both tried-and-true basic methods to get new quilters started, and more advanced techniques to help experienced quiltmakers expand their skills and boundaries.

I became a quilter about 20 years ago when I worked with Barbara Chainey, one of England's most talented hand quilters and teachers, on her first book, which I was editing. I was fascinated by terms Barbara used of which I had never heard ... like "rotary cutter." In an effort to educate myself in a crash course, I took a quilt-in-a-day workshop at Creative Quilting in southwest London. Quilters everywhere will sympathize with me when they learn that (a) I did not actually complete the quilt that day, and (b) it was many months later before I did finish it. But finish it I did, and I learned a lot of what I was seeking, and much more. My interest grew to a passion, and there are those (my husband among them) who consider my continuing interest more of an obsession, especially in my collection of old quilts.

A few quilts from the Gordon archive can be seen in Chapter 1, a brief illustrated history of quiltmaking. The book continues to a section of technical information outlining the basic methods used in this modern world for making quilts, including both hand and machine work. The following chapters cover the three basic areas of traditional quiltmaking: Patchwork, Appliqué, and Quilting. In each of these sections, a block or small project is created step-by-step in full color to show those new to the method how to make it. Included in these chapters are Tips and Notes, boxed for emphasis, to offer additional useful information about the technique itself, or a hint about making the task quicker, or a particular facet such as a special piece of equipment used in creating the block. Templates that can be used to recreate the designs are included in easily traceable form where they are relevant in a special section at the end of the book and cross-referenced for easy access. Cross-references are used throughout the book, and there is a full index at the end.

Measurements are given in specific projects in standard and metric measures. Always use one system or the other, because the conversions, while sometimes very close, are never exact, and mixing them can lead to errors that cause distortions in a finished block. And remember that the measurements given will lead to a block the same size as ours, but you can make your block any size you wish if you do your own calculations. My aim is not to have you create an exact copy of what is in the book, but to use it as a springboard to make your own ideas happen.

This book could not have been finished on schedule without the help of an enthusiastic team of stitchers, all talented and energetic members of my local quilt guild. They are, in alphabetical order, Tricia Glaister, Kathleen Golden, Karen Peck Katz, Pat Thompson Patza, Barbara Ritchey, Joanne Sook, Patsy Tighe, and Jane Walton. I thank them all from the bottom of my heart.

**THE QUILTERS**

*From left to right: Tricia Glaister, Barbara Ritchey, Kathleen Golden, Jane Walton, Maggi Gordon, Joanne Sook, Patsy Tighe, Karen Peck Katz, Pat Thompson Patza.*

# CHAPTER 1

# History

# History

*Quilts have been made for centuries, and the various needlework techniques employed by quiltmakers—patchwork, appliqué, and quilting—are practiced in almost every part of the world. The type and style of quilts change from place to place, climate to climate, culture to culture, but the methods are sometimes surprisingly similar. This book sets out to provide information and instructions for adapting the techniques, from the most widely practiced to less well-known but equally valid and interesting methods, to help the beginner and inspire the more experienced quiltmaker.*

**WHOLECLOTH**
*Dating from around 1870, the top of this white wholecloth quilt from Northeast England is made from a seersucker-like fabric and has a plain white cotton back. The quilting in the central area is a simple diamond grid, surrounded by a wide border of interlocking cables.*

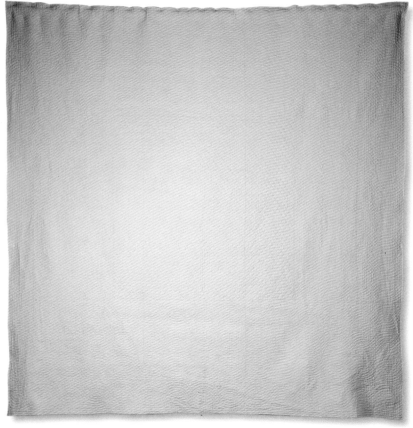

Quilts as bedcovers are of course the best-known form of the art. In the centuries before quilts migrated onto beds to sleep under, they provided nighttime warmth as hangings that surrounded the bed to keep out the cold drafts that blew through unheated homes. Quilting techniques were used to make garments, from ancient China and ancient Egypt, to the quilted jerkins and waistcoats worn by soldiers in the Middle Ages under their chain mail, to elegant ladies' petticoats and gentlemen's vests of the seventeenth and eighteenth centuries. Such clothing, highly fashionable, and the techniques used to make it, were taken to the American colonies by the early settlers, and the technical expertise traveled with the colonists as they moved deeper into the New World. Quilted clothing is still made today, both as designer fashion pieces and by ready-to-wear manufacturers, and the techniques can be employed by needleworkers to make one-off items to supplement their own wardrobes or those of their friends and family members.

The skills used to make clothing were soon adapted to make household items, especially quilts for beds. The majority of surviving antique quilts, starting from the late eighteenth and early nineteenth centuries through to the mid-twentieth century, are made from a variety of patchwork techniques, with substantial numbers of appliquéd examples dating from the middle of the nineteenth century. The technique that ties them all together, and indeed defines a "quilt," is quilting itself, in which the layers—most often the top, which can be plain, or pieced, or

**STRIPPY**

*Although the graphic red and white stripes in this Durham strippy quilt date from the 1880s, they could have been put together yesterday. Adjoining strips are quilted differently, with a diamond grid on the red stripes, and fans and cables alternating on the white. The original pencil lines marking the patterns is still visible in places.*

applied, the batting (wadding), or padding, in the middle, and the back or backing, which can be plain or pieced—are all stitched through to stabilize them and keep the central padding from shifting into the corners. But quilting is generally much more than a necessity. Quilting adds dimension and texture to the surface of a quilt, and the infinite variety of quilting patterns makes each quilt unique.

Among early examples of quilts are those referred to as "wholecloth," which are made from one large piece of fabric. Although the quilt may in fact be created from several pieces of fabric joined to make a top large enough for the purpose, the various pieces are from the same fabric and appear, especially once the quilting has been stitched, to be one large "whole" cloth. Many wholecloth quilts are made from solid-colored fabric, but there are also beautiful examples created from prints such as Indian chintz or paisley patterns. The backing is sometimes made from the same fabric as the front, but often the back is a different print or plain that creates a useful double-sided quilt. Wholecloth quilts were popular in the mid-nineteenth century, particularly in Britain and America, as well as in France, where they are known as "boutis." These French examples originated in the Mediterranean coastal area around Marseilles, and given the mild climate, are surprisingly thick and heavily padded, a combination of plain quilting and trapunto, or stuffed quilting.

Another similar type of quilt is the medallion or frame quilt. The term encompasses quilts that begin as a "medallion" in the center. This can be a quilting design worked on a wholecloth quilt and surrounded by a variety of other patterns, but most often refers to a quilt with a shape—usually square or rectangular but sometimes octagonal, for example—placed in the middle and outlined with a series of borders, some pieced, that frame the center.

A good number of wholecloth and medallion quilts were made in the area of the north of England around the counties of

Durham and Northumberland and along the Scottish border. However, that area is equally famous for its strippy quilts, made from several long strips of fabric joined lengthwise to make up the width of the quilt. During the second half of the nineteenth century, such quilts became known as "Durham strippies," and many of them were made by the wives and widows of coal miners in the area as a way to supplement a meager household income. By 1870 an early form of the layaway plan had developed: the so-called "quilt club" in which the buyer paid in installments. Strippies are made from prints or plains, with the most graphic pieced from two solid colors, one of which is often white or cream. The quilting can be done as an overall pattern, or can follow the strips in the form of rope, braid, cable, or twist patterns, and on the finest examples is highly elaborate, changing on each strip to a different pattern. Quilting on the "club" quilts tended to be simple, since time was of the essence for the maker.

The strippy, like other patterns, was taken to America, and like other patterns developed its own style. While British strippies seldom have a border or binding—-the edges are generally turned to the middle and double-stitched to enclose the batting—American versions often have borders and are usually bound with separate strips of fabric. Many examples from both countries include strips that are made from pieced blocks, and the highly graphic "bars" quilts, made by the Amish in solid colors but often with patchwork blocks comprising the strips and surrounded by wide borders, are thought to have been inspired by the Durham-type

**1000 PYRAMIDS**
*The fabrics in this quilt from Pennsylvania are typical of the 1880s, the era in which it was made. A few of the fabrics have been repeated, but the scraps are nearly all different, making it almost a charm quilt, in which no fabric is used more than once. The green and black printed backing fabric is also a fine example of its time.*

**HEXAGON FLOWERS**

*This stunning late Victorian mosaic quilt is a carefully planned combination of Grandmother's Flower Garden, based on hexagon rosettes, and Trip Around the World, in which concentric rings of color move out from the center. All the solid-colored flowers are made from a shiny satin fabric and set on a black background. The hexagonal area, created using the English paper piecing method, is mounted on modern black moire satin.*

*(Collection of Pat Thompson Patza.)*

strippies made by non-Amish (or "English") neighbors in Pennsylvania.

## Patchwork quilts

Patchwork as a technique has been around since humans first began to sew, though there are few surviving examples of textiles that would have been fragile even when they were first crafted and used. Most European social groups would have used patchwork methods to extend the life of valuable fabrics, and as societies became more settled and more skilled, scraps of cloth were joined together in patterns that were pleasing to the eye and enhanced the value of the newly created article.

## CRAZY QUILT

*This exuberant "contained crazy quilt" is one side (probably the back) of a double-sided quilt made in the late nineteenth century, possibly in Tennesse or Texas. The 15 blocks contain dozens of random scraps with some embroidered embellishment, and the whole quilt is tied at close intervals.*

By the middle of the nineteenth century, Victorian needleworkers in Britain and America were creating a variety of patchwork designs. A favorite technique, called English paper piecing, was used to make mosiac-effect quilts in geometric patterns from hexagons to triangles or diamonds. Many of these quilts were made from beautiful scraps of luxury fabrics left from dressmaking, as were the crazy quilts that were also popular at the time.

While the mosaic quilts depended upon the juxtaposition of light and dark color values for their drama, crazy quilts allowed a quiltmaker to use a huge variety

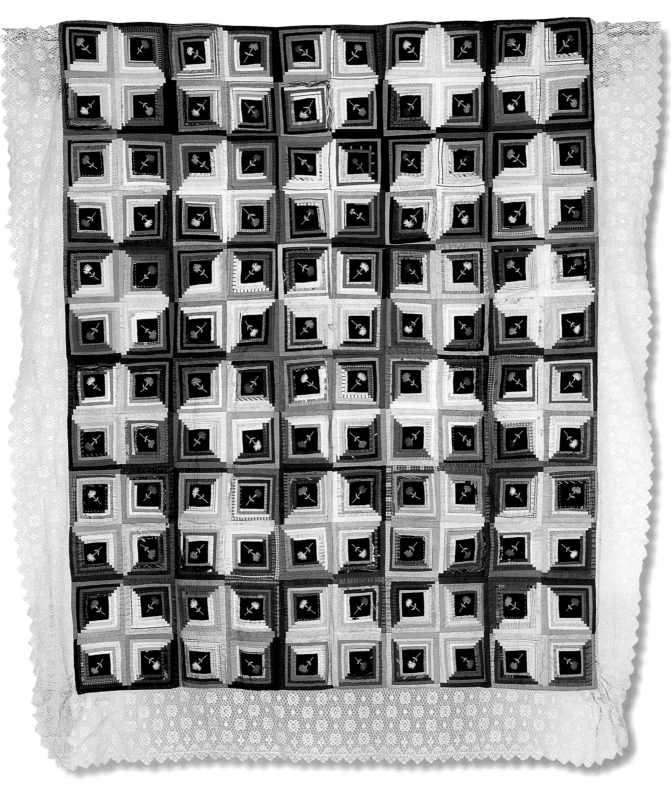

### LOG CABIN

*This beautiful and heavy Log Cabin quilt in a Light-and-Dark setting was most likely made in Yorkshire in the 1870s or '80s. Many of the silk strips are ribbons, and the center squares are black velvet, all embroidered with the same flower in different colors. It is bordered with a handmade lace border and batted with a blanket, or possibly another quilt.*

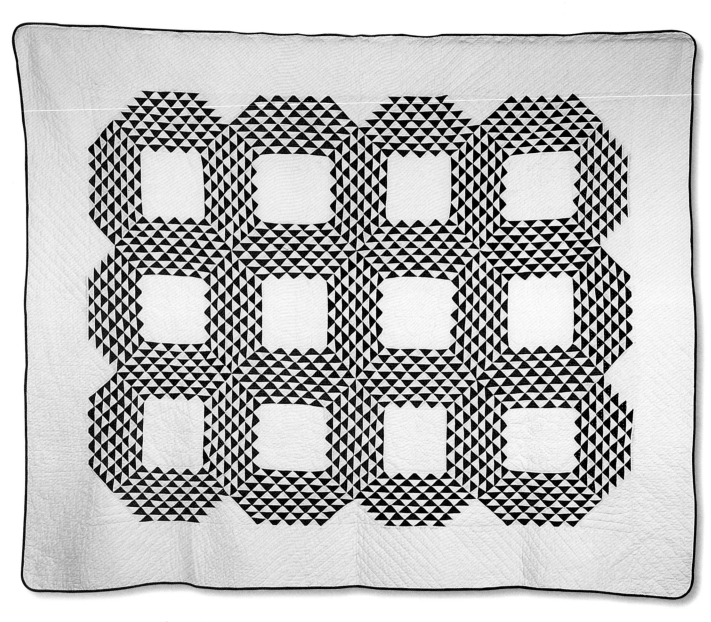

**OCEAN WAVES**
*This blue and white Ocean Waves patchwork quilt was made around 1900 in Indiana by an unknown quiltmaker. A variety of blue fabrics with tiny polka dots are teamed with the white background, and a flower has been quilted in each of the 8¹/2 in (22 cm) center squares.*

of unrelated fabrics that could be put together according to the shape of the scrap or the whim of the maker, and they were then embellished with embroidery, ribbons, buttons, beads, etc.

Patchwork patterns based on blocks also proliferated. One of the most widely made block designs was Log Cabin, which remains popular partly because of the simplicity of its construction and partly because of the almost infinite variety of possible combinations when the blocks are "set," or joined together, which almost

invariably creates new secondary patterns that obscure the outlines of the individual blocks. There were other blocks based on strips, and vast numbers based on squares, rectangles, triangles, and other shapes.

Block patchwork became almost synonomous with patchwork in the United States, where first the economy and then convenience played an important role in its popularity. In colonial times, fabric was all imported from Britain and was costly and precious. Patchwork blocks provided a way to husband all the scraps left from dressmaking and home sewing, and to recycle worn garments and household items. Storage space in the small homes, and later in frontier cabins as pioneers moved west, was limited, and blocks could be put away as they were finished until there were enough to make a quilt. Patterns and colors became more consistent and sophisticated as the young nation grew and prospered, and by the last half of the nineteenth century, patchwork quilts of great beauty were being created.

## Appliqué

The technique of applying a piece of one fabric to a larger background of a different cloth was used in Europe by the eighteenth century, but appliqué designs have been used to decorate all manner of items for much longer. Printed fabrics from the East, particularly India, began to be imported into Europe in the 1700s, and because it was expensive, the motifs were often cut out and applied to a plain background to make them more economical to use.

**ROBBING PETER TO PAY PAUL**
*Made in Delaware in about 1900 from a typical "double pink" fabric—a pale background color overprinted with a darker shade of pink—teamed with cream, this beautifully pieced quilt is at once traditional and modern-looking. The wreath, cable, and grid quilting is exquisite, and the markings can still be seen in a number of places.*

Appliqué lends itself to curved and intricate shapes that are hard to achieve in geometric patchwork designs. Among the best-known appliqué designs are found on a group of quilts made in and around Baltimore, Maryland, between the 1840s and the 1860s. Known as Baltimore Album quilts, they are brightly colored and carry designs from flowers and other botanical specimens to animals and buildings. Another group of quilts, known as Bible and Story quilts, show interpretations of biblical stories and folk tales as well as elaborate scenes of daily life and family histories, and there is an entire genre of quilts based on naive and charming folk-art designs. Appliquéd blocks were also popular for the same reasons as with patchwork blocks, and many fine examples

**BOXED FLOWER KIT**

*The appliquéd grid in which the sprays of bright pastel flowers are placed is an unusual feature of this 1930s kit quilt, allowing scope for elaborate quilting.*

**MOLA**

*The winged lizard was made in Panama in the mid-twentieth century in typically bright colors using the technique of reverse appliqué. The jagged teeth are appliquéd, while the lines on the head and back legs are embroidered in running stitch.*

*(Collection of Patricia Cox)*

exist of exquisitely worked traditional appliqué patterns and their variations.

In the early part of the twentieth century, a type of mainly appliqué quilts known as kit quilts developed. Stitchers could purchase a pattern to use with their own fabrics, or in some cases they could buy ready-printed fabrics that simply needed to be cut out and applied to the marked background. Most of these designs are floral, worked in the soft pastel colors that were widely available at the time.

**FLORAL APPLIQUÉ**
*This wonderful quilt with its elaborate flower border dates from around the time of the American Civil War. Both the double-pink and green fabrics are typical of the era, and the quilting is of the highest quality.*

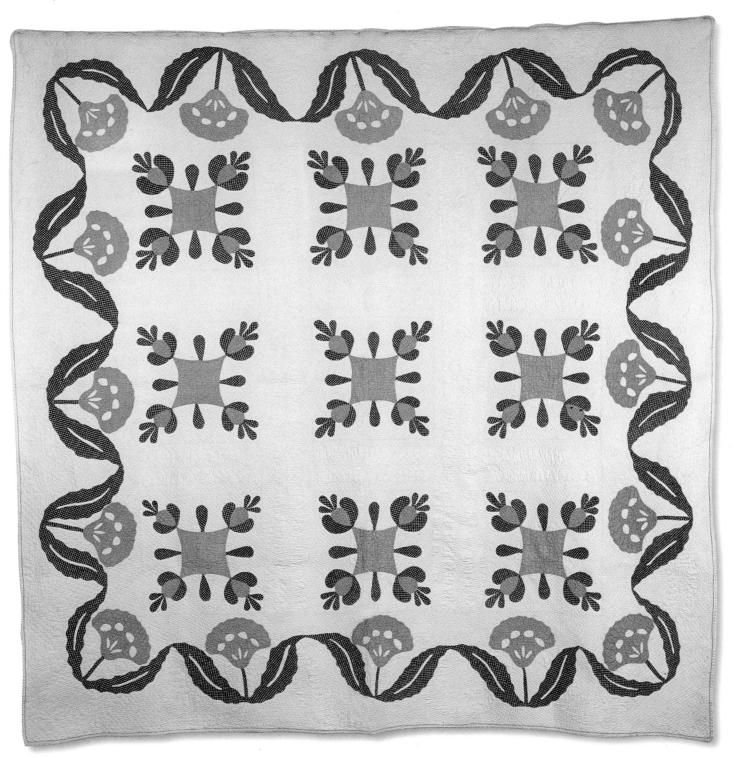

**AFRICAN-AMERICAN UTILITY**

*Made in 2003 by Annie B. Pettway of Gee's Bend, Alabama, this lively quilt takes its colors from the printed fabric. The pattern is an oversized Cabin in the Cotton block, a variation of Log Cabin, which is called "Housetop" by the local quiltmakers in the tiny community on the banks of the Alabama River. The backing is pieced cotton folded to the front to make the binding, and the quilting is worked in lines of big-stitch work.*

Appliqué with its flexibility and variety is widely used by today's art quilters and fabric artists. Most appliqué was traditionally worked by turning under a narrow strip of the raw edge and stitched as invisibly as possible. A technique known as reverse appliqué also exists, in which fabrics are layered and a design is cut into the top fabric, which is turned under and stitched down to reveal the layer behind it. This technique was perfected on opposite sides of the globe among two different tribal groups, the islanders of the San Blas islands of Panama and the Hmong of Indochina, and has been adopted by quiltmakers around the world.

## Quilting

There is a saying that quilting makes the quilt. Certainly, the texture that is added by quilting any quilt creates a piece that looks entirely different if it is not quilted, and a traditional design can enhance a patchwork or appliqué pattern immeasurably. But there are several specialized types of quilting that are also highly valued by today's quiltmakers. Corded or Italian quilting, which consists of pulling a cord or string through a narrow channel stitched in the chosen design, is the technique used on one of the oldest bed quilts in existence—the Tristram quilt at the Victoria and Albert Museum in London. A related technique is trapunto, or stuffed quilting, in which a layer of thin fabric is placed on the wrong side of the quilt top and stuffing is inserted into the spaces created by the quilted pattern to make raised or padded areas. This method is seen at its zenith in the boutis quilts from France mentioned earlier, but it is found on many antique quilts and is a favorite technique of modern quilters, especially with the advent of machine-worked trapunto.

Utility quilting is widely seen, particularly on everyday quilts. Tying is one method that falls into this category. Quilts are tied by threading a piece of yarn or thread through all the layers, bringing it back to the top, and tying a double knot to hold it, then cutting the thread and moving to another spot. Because it is a quick method, it was widely used on pioneer quilts and is found on many African-American examples. The big stitches that are associated with utility quilting are also widely seen on African-American quilts, where they create wonderful, seemingly random patterns. Sashiko quilting is a Japanese variation of utility quilting, but unlike its more relaxed American counterpart, it relies on even stitches and spaces to create wonderful geometric and pictorial designs.

Both hand quilting and machine quilting require patience and practice to execute well, and there are large numbers of quilts in existence that show the skill of their makers. Traditional hand quilting is found on most antique quilts, but the sewing machine and the long-arm quilting machine are being used by more and more quiltmakers. Many of tomorrow's antiques will be machine quilted.

# CHAPTER 2

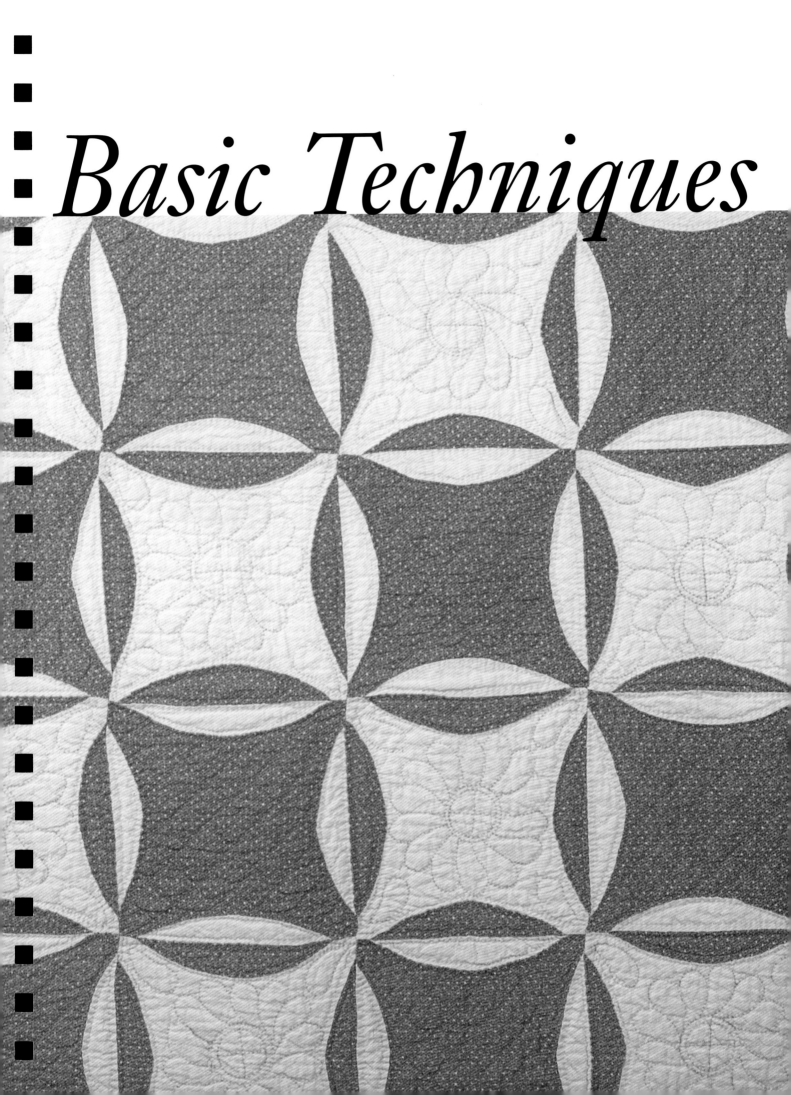

# Basic Techniques

**WOOL AND LINEN**
*Wool and linen are usually plain. Patterns like stripes and checks are generally woven into the fabric, and the printed wool shown below is unusual.*

# About fabric

*Although many different materials are used to make quilts these days, quilters mainly make their creations from fabric. Choosing the appropriate fabrics can be a confusing minefield, and it is crucial to the outcome.*

Fabrics made from natural fibers are generally best for quiltmaking, both for pieced and applied work, and for quilting. Natural fabrics—cotton, wool, silk, and linen —are comfortable to handle and easy to stitch. Many desirable-looking fabrics are either blends of natural and synthetic fibers, or 100 percent synthetic, but they tend to be harder to fold and press, and quilting them by hand is not as easy or as satisfying as working on natural-fiber materials.

Cotton is by far the most widely used fabric for quiltmaking. Woven from the soft white fibers of the cotton plant, which grows in many warm-weather areas of the world, cotton is available in a variety of weights and weaves. It takes dye well, either with designs printed on the finished cloth, or when cotton thread or yarn is predyed to be woven into patterns like plaids or checks. It feels good to touch, washes well, and is easy to press, and it should be the only choice for quilts intended for babies and small children. Like most fibers, cotton can shrink when washed, so, as with most fabric, it is best to wash it before starting on a project.

## using silk for quilts

The luxury of silk makes it a desirable fabric for quiltmaking, but its special problems, such as its tendency to fray and to slip about as you work, mean that it should be handled with care and attention. It is a strong material that can be found in a huge variety of weights and weaves, from heavy slubbed close weaves to gossamer sheers, woven into velvet, satin, taffeta, brocade, and organdy that create wonderful effects when they are cut and combined.

Wool is another popular natural fabric, used for quiltmaking more in days gone by, when wool for spinning and for batting was easy to obtain in the cold climates from which much quiltmaking originated, than in today's centrally heated homes. It has a traditional look and feel that makes it very satisfying to work with. Wool quilts are warm and cozy, but except in lightweight weaves, the fabric can be difficult and heavy to use for making quilts.

Silk and linen are both used for quiltmaking, but since both need careful handling – they fray easily and are harder to clean – and are generally more expensive than cotton or wool, they are found less often in quilts made today. It is their tendency to fray that causes most problems, especially among inexperienced quiltmakers. However, silk in particular creates special effects that cannot be duplicated by any other fabric. It has enormous strength and can be woven into a wide variety of weights and weaves from gossamer sheers to heavily slubbed tight weaves. It is easy to cut and to press, and when pieces are cut and turned in different directions, the play of light on the surface makes the color seem to be another color altogether.

The sheen of silk is unlike any other, and handling silk, especially when quilting, say, a wholecloth bed cover is a luxurious pleasure for anyone who loves fabric. The various luxury fabrics, most of them based on silk, like velvet, satin, organdy, taffeta, and brocade, can be used to create wonderfully visual and creative textural effects, but they all need careful handling.

Linen is probably the least-used natural fiber for quiltmaking. It has a coarseness when compared to the other naturals, and it is prone to wrinkles and creases that can be hard to remove.

> tip: FABRIC GRAIN
> All fabric has three "grains," or directions of woven threads. The lengthwise threads, the "warp," are strung on the loom, with the "weft" threads crossing them horizontally in and out, under and over. The rigid edges on each side of a length of fabric are called "selvages." The diagonal grain is the "bias." The warp and weft threads remain fairly stationary under tension, but the bias, which has more give and elasticity, stretches more easily and must be handled carefully.

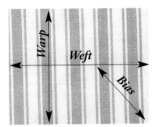

## COTTON
*Cotton fabrics come in an astonishing variety of weights, weaves, and patterns, from geometric stripes, plaids, and checks to printed designs.*

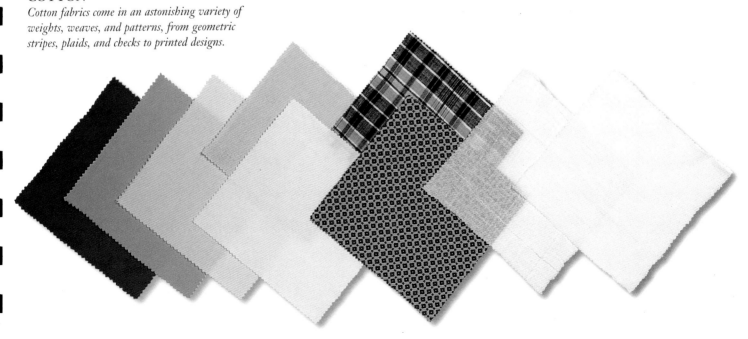

# About color

*The colors in a quilt are the crucial element in its design. Color is a highly technical and complicated subject, about which many books have been written, and quiltmakers need to be familiar with the basic aspects of the theory.*

The first element in color theory is that there are three primary colors—red, yellow, and blue. From these basics all other colors can be created, although the neutrals of black and white must also be introduced in some cases. Primary colors can be placed in a circle known as a color wheel, and when analogous colors—those that appear side by side—are combined, new colors, known as secondary colors, are made. So, blue and yellow make green, yellow and red make orange, and red and blue make purple. When a secondary is combined with its adjoining primary, yet another hue, called a tertiary or intermediate color, occurs. Adding black or white to any color creates a shading that can be used to great advantage in quiltmaking.

*Yellow and two shades of orange are examples of analogous colors.*

## complementary colors

Colors that appear on opposite sides of the color wheel are known as complementary colors. At the simplest level, they are blue and orange, red and green, and yellow and purple. They can be combined to create a lively, somewhat unexpected effect that is used in many areas of design and home decorating.

# Color and pattern

*One of the most difficult aspects of quiltmaking for many people is visualizing how fabrics will look once they have been cut into pieces and reassembled. Experience can be valuable, and many quiltmakers like to stick to "the rules," at least in the beginning.*

Value—the lightness or darkness of a fabric —is perhaps the most important aspect in juxtaposing colors. In fact, the value of a fabric is sometimes more important than its actual color, and the perceived value of a fabric depends to a certain extent, sometimes crucially, on the color of the fabric placed next to it. Because it can be hard to imagine what will happen when colors have been combined and shapes stitched together, it is a good idea to make a small sample if possible to judge the effect. A good way to practice assessing value is to assemble a set of monochromatic fabrics— all the same color but in different patterns, shades, and tints—and grade them from light to dark.

The scale, or size of the image, of a pattern is also important to its successful use in quiltmaking. Generally, small-scale prints work best, although larger patterns can be used to create wonderful effects, especially if they are combined with plain fabrics.

*Monochromatic (left) and light-to-dark (below) color schemes are both useful approaches to using color in quiltmaking.*

## Patterned and plain fabrics

Combining patterned and plain fabric can give visual texture to a piece of work and create a highly desirable contrast. Pay careful attention to all the aspects of color selection, such as value, when you are choosing fabrics.

## Scale

The scale of the pattern, particularly in patchwork, must be considered carefully. Smaller-scale prints are usually more successful since they can be cut into small units without losing their identity.

## two-color combinations

Combining two highly contrasted colors gives a visual richness that is hard to achieve in any other way. They can be shades from the same color family but with completely different values, one very light and the other very dark.

Navy blue and white, as shown here, is a popular combination, as are red and white or black and white. A white background will make a bright primary color stand out vividly, and while two pastels won't have enough contrast to make successful designs, if a lighter pastel color is combined with black, it can glow like a jewel. Equal amounts of each color can fool the eye and create wonderful optical illusions.

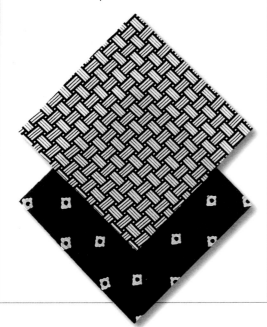

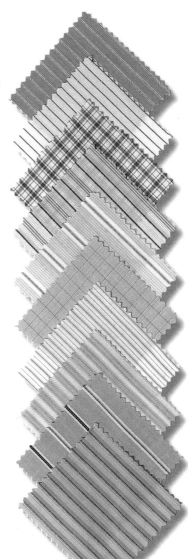

## Geometric patterns

Geometric patterns—checks, stripes, or plaids—can be juxtaposed effectively, or they can be combined with other patterned or solid-colored fabrics. These patterns are widely used in country-style quilts with great effect.

# Tools and equipment

*Quiltmakers, like dressmakers, have worked for centuries with a minimum of basic equipment. The only real necessities are probably scissors, pins and needles, simple measuring and marking tools, thread, and perhaps a thimble. However, there is an astonishing range of specialized equipment, some of it designed for a specific task and some adapted from other skills, available for the avid quiltmaker to choose from today.*

## Measuring and marking equipment

Although there is a vast choice of specialized measuring tools for the quiltmaker, the basic set, from simple rulers and measuring tapes to set squares and flexible curves, can be found in a desk or workshop.

Much marking equipment is also part of most home offices, but there are also many specific quilt-marking tools available, from water-soluble pens to special chalks and crayons.

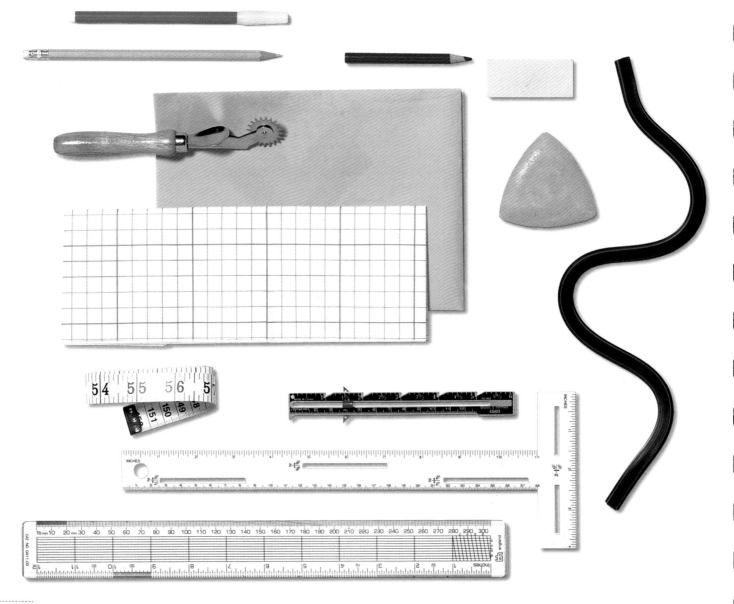

## Templates and stencils

Templates are used mainly in patchwork and appliqué, while stencils are widely used for marking quilting designs on quilt tops. Ready-made metal or plastic templates come in a wide array of styles and sizes. They can be expensive to purchase, but they are highly accurate and long-lasting, ideal for a major project, especially when bias seams are involved. One type consists of a pair of similar templates, one solid for cutting backing papers and marking seam allowances, the other ¼ in (5 mm) larger with a "window" for viewing the fabric.

Quilting stencils are usually made of translucent plastic and also last well. You can make your own templates and stencils from sheets of template plastic or thin cardboard.

## Sewing equipment

For hand stitching patchwork, appliqué, or quilting, sewing equipment is always a personal choice. Some people use safety pins instead of straight pins. Many stitchers use a thimble when sewing by hand, and hand quilters swear by them—many use one on each hand, both to protect their digits from being stabbed and their quilts from being bloodied. Needles come in many types and sizes, from "betweens," the most common hand quilting and appliqué needle, to "sharps" for general sewing, to various kinds of embroidery and milliners' needles. Needles come in various sizes; experiment to find which you prefer.

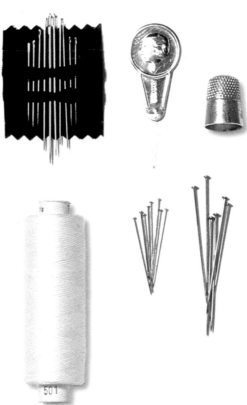

## Cutting equipment

While scissors are a basic cutting tool, essential for cutting curves, trimming seams, and clipping threads, the most important change in quiltmaking over the past generation is without a doubt the rotary cutter and its companion tools, the rotary ruler and the self-healing cutting mat. Most of us would be lost without these timesavers, which speed up the tedious cutting-out process by allowing us to cut several layers at once with accuracy. The strips we cut can be chain-pieced (see page 42), so the time it takes to make a quilt is shortened dramatically.

But keep those scissors handy: one pair for cutting fabric, one for paper and batting, and a pair of small thread snippers.

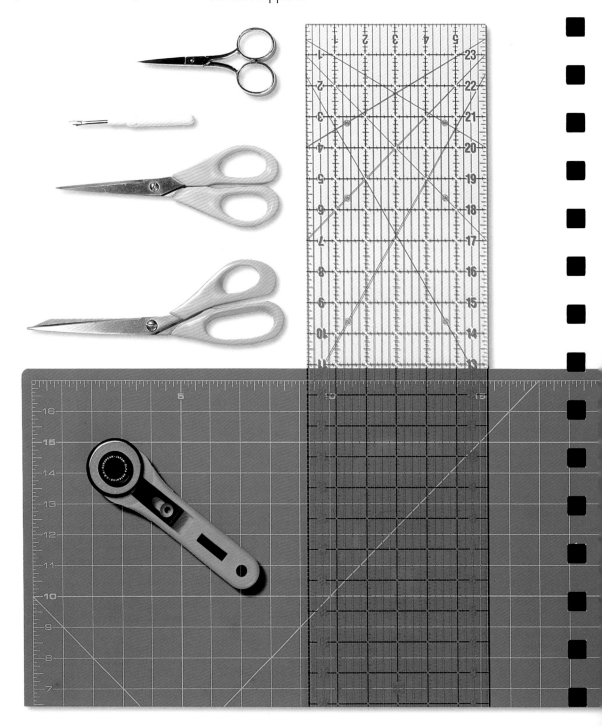

## Sewing machines

All sewing machines have certain features in common, but they are all slightly different. The best way to become familiar with what your sewing machine can do, and the way it works, is to try out the various functions and experiment with various feet and attachments on different thicknesses of fabric and batting. If you have a new machine, or feel rusty, attend a class that concentrates on your type of machine—many suppliers offer these workshops. Learning from someone who is highly familiar with your particular machine is especially important with the new generation of computerized machines, several of which are designed to be particularly useful to quiltmakers.

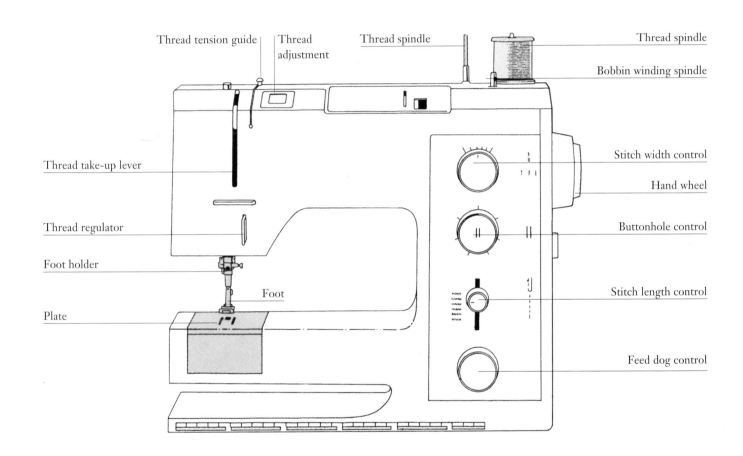

Thread tension guide | Thread adjustment | Thread spindle | Thread spindle | Bobbin winding spindle | Thread take-up lever | Stitch width control | Hand wheel | Thread regulator | Buttonhole control | Foot holder | Foot | Stitch length control | Plate | Feed dog control

### BALANCED STITCH
*The two threads join the middle of the layers of fabric and look the same on both sides. to check the tension is correct, test a row of stitching on a scrap of the fabric you are using before starting work.*

### BOTTOM THREAD IS TOO TIGHT
*If the bottom thread lies in a line and the top one shows through the back of the seam, loosen the bobbin thread carefully, as recommended by the instruction manual. Usually a screw in the bobbin case.*

### TOP THREAD IS TOO TIGHT
*If the top thread lies in a line and the bobbin thread is visible on the top of the seam, loosen the needle thread using the thread adjustment control, following the manufacturer's instructions.*

# Marking and cutting

*Cutting out pieces accurately for patchwork or appliqué is crucial to the look of the finished piece. Cutting by hand is the time-honored traditional way used by generations of quiltmakers.*

Using scissors is the best method for cutting out shapes with curves since bias edges can easily be pulled out of true. Scissors that are suitable for quiltmaking come in an almost unimaginable selection of types and sizes, from small pairs for cutting thread and clipping seam allowances to large, very sharp dressmaking shears that should be used only to cut fabric. In between are scissors to cut paper, template plastic, and synthetic batting, which can become dull quickly and should never be used on cloth. There is also a vast array of highly specialized scissors from pinking shears used most often in dressmaking to those decided specifically for left-handed quiltmakers.

## MAKING TEMPLATES

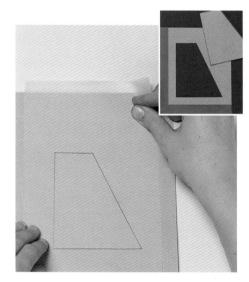

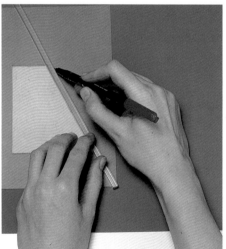

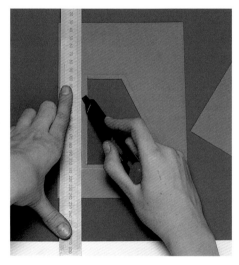

1 Irregular shapes can be cut more easily if you create a template. Trace the required shape to the correct size and glue the tracing securely to a piece of cardboard. Inset: cut the shape out precisely.

2 Place the cardboard template on a sheet of template plastic and draw around the shape. To make a window template, add a ¼ in (5mm) seam allowance around all sides of the template—here, we have used a quilter's quarter for accuracy.

3 Using a craft knife and metal ruler, carefully cut out the inner "window" and then the extended template around the outside edge. The inner "window" can be used to mark the stitching line as well as the support papers, if these are used, while the outer section can be used for cutting fabric patches to the correct size.

## PAPER PATTERNS

1 Some shapes are easier to cut using a paper pattern like a dressmaker's pattern. Pin the pattern to the fabric, aligning at least one straight edge with the fabric grain unless the pattern specifies otherwise. You do not need to cut out the paper pattern first—in fact, it can be easier to follow the cutting line marked on the paper than to cut precisely around an edge that has already been cut.

2 Unless your fabric is very thick, you can cut multiples of two or more layers at once. Lay the fabric so the grain is straight on all the pieces and pin through all layers. Make sure your scissors are very sharp. The excess paper will fall away with the cut-off fabric.

## CUTTING FROM WINDOW TEMPLATES

1 This method is often used to cut the fabric and the backing papers for English paper piecing (see page 41). Fabric shapes are mounted on backing papers cut ¼ in (5 mm) smaller. This is the finished size of the patch. Mark paper shapes using the inside line of the window template and cut a paper for each patch required.

2 Place the template on the fabric and align the grain where possible. Draw around the template, inside and out, being careful not to drag the marker along the fabric, which might cause stretching. The outer line is the cutting line; the inner line shows the finished size.

3 Cut out each fabric piece along the outside line, using sharp fabric scissors to minimize stretching and fraying.

# Rotary cutting

*Rotary cutting is a method based on updated technology and our perceived need for speed in all things. You can rotary-cut strips to join in sequence individual patches with straight sides, from squares and rectangles to various triangles.*

Rotary rulers and cutters come in a huge selection of sizes and shapes these days, in a variety of lengths and widths. When working with these tools, always align and measure the fabric with either the ruler or the mat—never both—and cover the part of the fabric which you will be using with the ruler to avoid cutting into it. Always cut away from yourself. If possible, experiment with the various types of cutters, rulers, and mats in classes and workshops to decide which ones best suit your needs.

## safety first!

To cut easily and accurately, rotary cutters must have extremely sharp blades. All cutters have safety guards, and you should establish the habit of setting the guard after every cut you make to avoid nasty accidents. If a blade becomes dull and no longer cuts through the full length of the fabric completely, replace it immediately. Always cut away from your body, and use a self-healing cutting mat both to protect your work surface and to prolong the life of your cutter blades.

## ROTARY CUTTING

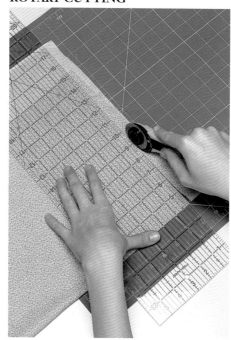

1 Fold the washed and pressed fabric along the straight grain to fit on the cutting mat. Level off the edge to be cut. Place the ruler over the "good" fabric and hold it steady while you trim away the uneven edge.

2 Turn the fabric over so the ruler covers the area you want to end up with. Measure the width of strip that you need and cut along the grain, usually from selvage to selvage.

## CUTTING PIECED STRIPS

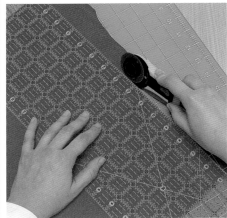

1 The speed of working with rotary-cut strips comes from the fact that they can be stitched together in a sequence and then cut again to be reassembled into different patterns.

Stitch strips together and press the seams to one side. Lay the pieced strip right side up on the mat, align the ruler across its width, and cut pieced strips of the desired width.

2 The procedure is similar if you wish to cut strips at an angle to the seams. Cut the end of the pieced strips to the desired angle—here it is 45 degrees—and line up the ruler and measure from the angled edge.

## CUTTING A BIAS STRIP

1 To cut bias strips accurately, lay the fabric on the mat, and with the ruler covering the "good" material, cut across the width to make a straight edge.

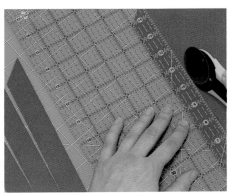

3 Using the edge cut in Step 2 as the guideline, cut strips of the desired width, always covering the intended strip with the ruler.

2 Measure a 45-degree angle in one corner of the fabric and cut across that corner to make a short edge on the true bias.

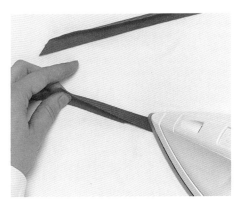

4 If the strips will be used as some form of binding, press—do NOT iron— each strip in half lengthwise. Do not stretch the strip out of shape as you work.

## Rotary rulers and mats:

Rotary rulers are made from clear acrylic and marked in a 1-in (2.5-cm) grid, usually in ¼-in (5 mm) or ⅛-in (2.5-mm) increments. Rulers can be rectangular, square, or triangular in 45-degree or 60-degree configurations, and there are a number of specially designed rulers for cutting stars, diamonds, plates and fan blades, and other specialty shapes. Geometric shapes such as hexagons can also be cut using specialty rulers.

Mats also come in a variety of sizes and are marked, like the rulers, in 1-in (2.5-cm) grids divided into ⅛-in (2.5 mm) increments.

# Hand piecing

*While many patterns can be stitched more quickly by machine, piecing by hand is the best method for others, and some stitchers prefer hand sewing for its tactile qualities.*

Small patches, some curved patterns, and pieces with bias seams can often be stitched more easily and accurately by hand than by machine. Patches can be joined with running stitch or backstitch. The seamline should be marked and pinned carefully before you sew. Do not stitch into the seam allowances in case you need to trim them later.

Although various ways of working the patterns associated with paper piecing (see page 41) by machine have been devised, the method, which is used to assemble such familiar patterns as Grandmother's Flower Garden based on hexagons and Tumbling Blocks based on diamonds, is traditionally worked by hand. Window templates (see pages 36–37) are used to cut backing papers and fabric shapes.

**STRAIGHT SEAMS**

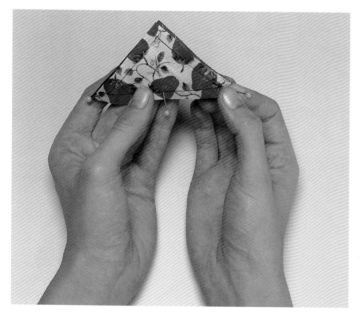

1 With right sides together, pin the patches along the seam to be stitched, matching the corners carefully. We have pinned each corner and the center; larger pieces may need more pins.

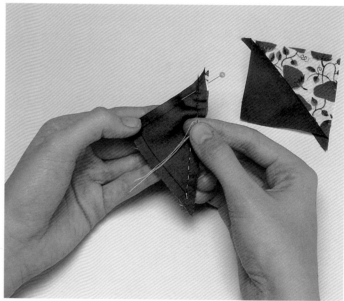

2 Sew along the marked seam, beginning and ending precisely at the corners. Handle bias seams with care to avoid stretching the fabric.

## FOUR-PIECE SEAMS

1 Join two contrasting patches along the marked stitching line. Repeat and press the seams to one side.

2 Pin the two units right sides together, first pushing a pin through the center seam to mark it precisely.

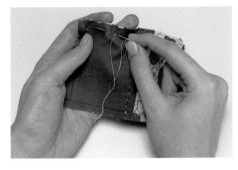

3 Work from the center out to join the two units, first along one side, then the other.

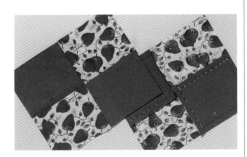

4 Seen from the right side (left), the corners of the block meet precisely in the center.

## ENGLISH PAPER PIECING

1 Cut a backing paper and a fabric shape for each unit, and pin a backing paper to the wrong side of each fabric patch. Fold the seam allowance over the edge of the paper and baste it in place, starting on the right side of the fabric—if the knot is on the right side, it is easier to remove the basting threads later.

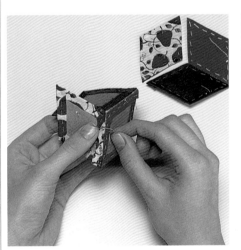

3 Match the point of a third patch to the inside of the center seam and align each corner. Work from the center out to complete the block.

2 Place two basted patches right sides together and make sure the corners are level. Whipstitch the edges of the pieces together, making sure you do not stitch through the papers. All the papers should be left in place until all the blocks have been joined.

tip: SET-IN SEAMS Hand piecing is especially useful for setting in patches with sharp angles, such as the Tumbling Block shown here, front and back.

# Machine piecing

*The sewing machine was invented in the early 1800s, and since the 1840s, hand-turned and then treadle machine have been used by quiltmakers. Electric machines are available in many versions, including computerized editions that carry out a wide variety of sewing tasks.*

Strip-piecing forms the basis for the majority of patchwork patterns that are popular today. The speed of cutting and sewing strips together to be cut and re-stitched appeals to modern quiltmakers, but accuracy is essential. If you make a mistake in measuring the size of a seam allowance, for example, you will end up with blocks of different sizes that do not fit together properly. Most machines can be fitted with a special foot that measures a precise ¼ in (5 mm) seam, but if you do not have one, you can mark the needle plate with a piece of masking tape laid the correct distance from the needle.

Chain-piecing speeds up the process even more. In this method, you sew in a continuous line, feeding prepared patches through the machine without lifting the foot or breaking the thread. The resulting chain of units is held together by short lengths of thread, which are cut apart once all the elements have been stitched.

Triangle squares are created from right-angle triangles sewn along the long side to create square units. There are various quick methods for making them.

Curved seams need careful preparation before being machine stitched. Mark the seamline on the wrong side of the pieces to be joined before pinning and stitching.

**STRIPS**

To join strips, place them right sides together, lining up the raw edges, and make a straight ¼ in (5mm) seam down the entire length. Make sure the seam allowances are even and the stitching line is straight. Press the seam toward the darker fabric. The joined strip can be cut into pieced units and combined in a variety of ways.

**CHAIN PIECING**

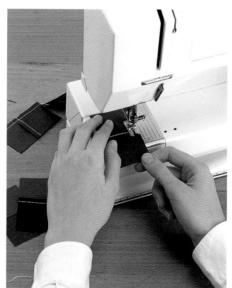

1 Place the units within reach and feed them through the machine one after the other without lifting the foot or breaking the thread

2 Cut apart the resulting units, which are held together by short threads.

## PIECED UNITS

1 To combine pieced units, press the seams of each unit to one side, alternating them so that when two units are placed right sides together, the pressed seams face in opposite directions. Align the raw edges and stitch a ¹⁄₄ in (5 mm) seam.

2 The joined units have evenly matched rows with squared-up corners at each meeting point (front and back).

## CURVED SEAMS

1 Pin the curved edges to be stitched with the pins at right angles to the raw edge. Pin the center first, then each end, then pin in between as needed for stability.

2 Stitch along the marked seamline, removing pins as you work.

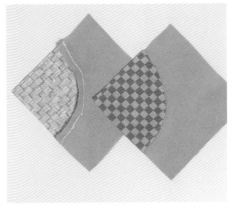

3 Press the seam toward the concave edge so that it lies flat.

## MAKING TRIANGLE SQUARES

1 Cut two contrasting strips the same width. On the wrong side of the lighter strip, mark squares the same measurement as the strip.

Mark a diagonal line in the first square in one direction, then alternate the direction in the adjacent square. Mark half as many squares as you need this way—each square will make two triangle squares. With right sides of the strips together, stitch along one side of the diagonal lines, ¹⁄₄ in (5mm) away. Because the diagonals alternate, you will be able to continue stitching down the length of the strip. When you reach the end, stitch each square ¹⁄₄ in (5mm) from the opposite side of the diagonal line working in the other direction.

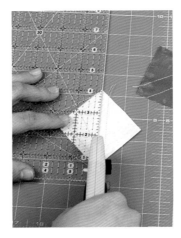

2 Use a rotary cutter to cut the squares apart. Then cut along the marked diagonal lines.

3 Open the squares and press the seams to the darker side. Trim the tails at the ends of the seams to square up the shapes.

# Hand appliqué

*Appliqué is the art of stitching cut-out shapes to a background fabric to create a new design. There are many ways of working appliqué.*

The most traditional method of working appliqué by hand is known as turned-edge or needle-turned appliqué. The motif to be applied is generally cut with a narrow seam allowance and either pinned or basted in place, then slipstitched or blindstitched on the background fabric. Baste rather than pin unless you are an experienced appliqué practitioner. Plain-weave natural fabrics are preferred for turned-edge appliqué since blends and knitted fabrics do not turn under as easily.

Freezer paper, widely used in appliqué work, originated as a supermarket item. It was designed to wrap food for the freezer, but quiltmakers discovered that its paper side could be drawn on and the plastic-coated side could be ironed on fabric to stabilize it. It can be used in a variety of ways in making quilts and is especially useful in appliqué work.

Bias strips are found in much appliqué, from stained glass patterns to Celtic work. It is possible to purchase bias strips with an iron-on backing that can then be sewn in place, but if you want to match a fabric or create a particular effect, you can make your own successfully.

**TURNED-EDGE APPLIQUÉ: METHOD 1**

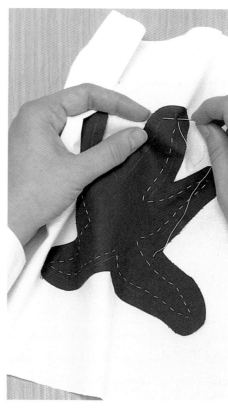

1 Make a template for the motif and draw around it lightly on the right side of the fabric.

2 Cut out the fabric shape, leaving approximately ¼ in (5 mm) of seam allowance all around.

3 Baste the wrong side of the shape to the right side of the background fabric using contrasting thread. Use small stitches and work approximately ¼ in (5 mm) inside the marked line.

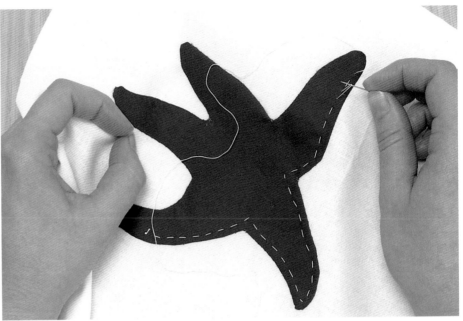

4 Use the end of the needle to turn the raw edge under, a little at a time, to abut the basted line, and slipstitch or blindstitch the folded edge to the background using thread to match the shape.

5 Remove the basting carefully and press gently from the wrong side.

6 The edges of the finished appliqué will be smooth.

# alternative technique:

**TURNED-EDGE APPLIQUÉ: METHOD 2**

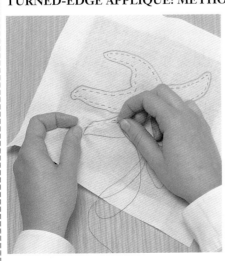

1 Use the template to draw around the shape on the wrong side of the background fabric. Remember that the shape will appear in reverse on the right side. Cut a piece of appliqué fabric larger all around than the motif and pin it in place, wrong side to the right side of the background and covering the drawn shape. Working from the wrong side of the background, use contrasting thread to baste it in place, sewing approximately ⅛ in (3 mm) inside the drawn line.

2 Turn the piece to the right side and cut out the shape with fabric scissors, approximately ¼ in (5 mm) from the basted line. Proceed as in Steps 4 and 5 above.

## TURNED-EDGE APPLIQUÉ: FREEZER-PAPER METHOD

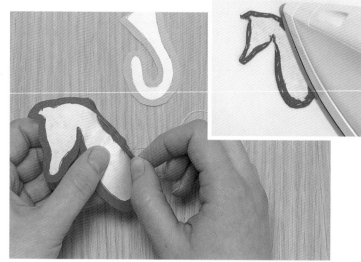

**1** Trace each element of the design separately on the paper side of freezer paper. Reverse the design, or the motif will be the wrong way around. Cut out each piece and iron it on the wrong side of the chosen fabric.

**2** Cut around the paper shapes, leaving ¼ in (5 mm) seam allowances all around.

**3** Turn the raw edges to the wrong side and baste them in place, clipping into the seam allowance if necessary. If an edge will be hidden by another piece, do not fold or baste it. Inset: Press the basted edge from the wrong side.

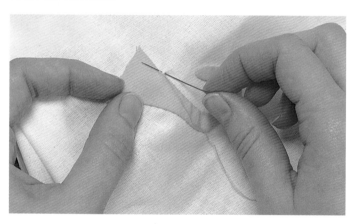

**4** Position the first piece on the background and pin it in place. Slipstitch around the folded edges using thread to match the piece.

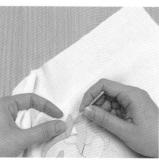

**5** Here, the top edge of the tail piece will be hidden by the body, so it can be left open and the paper removed.

**6** Apply the next piece in the same way. Start stitching in a place that will make it easier to leave an opening through which to remove the paper, and finish stitching after the paper has been removed.

**7** If the paper cannot be removed from the top, make a small slit in the background fabric and slip the paper piece through to remove it.

## BIAS STRIPS

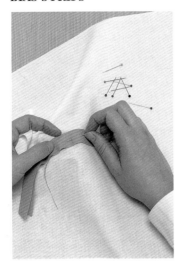 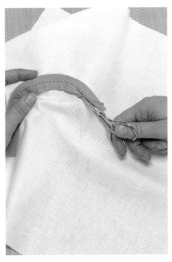  

**1** Cut a bias strip a little longer than necessary and 1½ in (3 cm) wide. With wrong sides together, press it in half lengthwise. Do not iron it—this will stretch the fabric. Pin the strip in place on the background.

**2** Use small running stitches to sew along the center of the strip, easing around curves gently as you go. Trim the raw edges ⅛ in (3 mm) from the stitching line.

**3** Turn the doubled strip over the stitched line and slipstitch it in place along the folded edge, covering the stitched line as you work.

**4** Turn under any raw ends that will show and slipstitch them in place. Ends that will be covered by another piece can be left unfinished.

## Making Peaks and valleys

Peaks and valleys—sharp points and corresponding troughs, or dips—occur on most appliqué shapes. Various tricks can be used to work them smoothly.

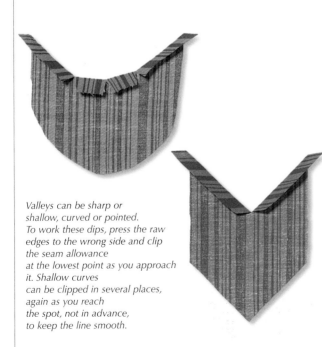

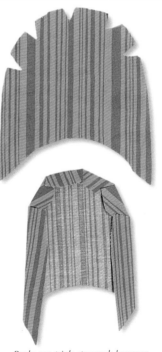 

*Valleys can be sharp or shallow, curved or pointed. To work these dips, press the raw edges to the wrong side and clip the seam allowance at the lowest point as you approach it. Shallow curves can be clipped in several places, again as you reach the spot, not in advance, to keep the line smooth.*

*Peaks are tricky to work because they inevitably have surplus fabric in the seam allowance that must be removed VERY CAREFULLY. Cutting notches in the*

*allowance of curved "hills" makes it easier to turn the edge under, while removing the very tip of a sharp point means it can be folded under neatly.*

# Machine appliqué

*The sewing machine is a useful modern tool for applied work, capable of creating interesting results.*

A machine with a zigzag function is essential, and many machines have a selection of decorative built-in embroidery stitches that can be used to outline and embellish machine appliqué work. If you have an open embroidery or appliqué foot, use it—it will be easier to see what is happening as you work.

There are several ways to hold pieces in place as you stitch around them. Pinning and basting can be used, but pins need to be removed as you approach them, and basting can sometimes get caught in the foot. Using craft or fabric glue, or aerosol basting spray, creates a firm but temporary bond, which means the piece can be repositioned before stitching

if necessary, and both adhesives should wash out. Fusible web is a fabric-bonding material consisting of a paper side that can be drawn on, with a thin layer of glue on the other side that is activated by ironing it in place. Its bond is permanent, and creates a slight stiffness in the areas where it is used.

Pieces to be applied by machine do not need seam allowances because the stitching is done along the raw edges, and machine appliqué can be an effective way to work broderie perse (see pages 110–111). Before embarking on a piece of work, make a test swatch to be sure the stitch length and width are suitable and the tension is correct.

## MACHINE APPLIQUÉ

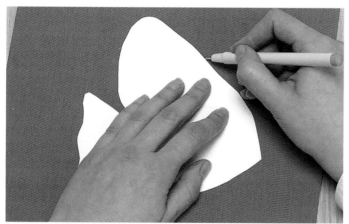

1 Make a template for each piece and draw around it on the chosen fabric. Make sure the template is the right way up or the piece will be reversed. Cut out the piece.

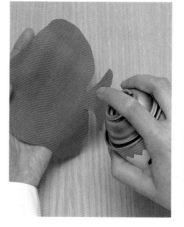

2 Spray the wrong side of the piece with a light coat of basting spray.

3 Position the shape on the background fabric

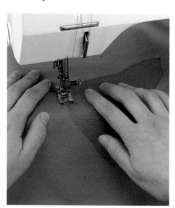

4 Set the machine for the desired stitch and do a test. Begin stitching in a place that can be hidden by the stitching or covered by another piece and work around the shape.

5 A close zigzag or satin stitch has been used here, but other decorative stitches are also appropriate.

# Hand quilting

*Quilting by hand has been practiced in different forms for thousands of years in culture worldwide. A technique that probably began as a way to hold layers of clothing together for warmth developed into a decorative art that has been handed down in places around the globe, from the kantha work of South Asian seamstresses in Bangladesh and the ralli and saami quilts of Pakistan and western India to the boutis of southern France and the wholecloth quilts of northeastern England.*

Quilting has appeared on European clothing and home furnishings since the sixteenth century, and the techniques traveled to the far corners of the world with each wave of exporation and immigration. Traditional Western quilting is worked through three layers: the top, which can be plain (or wholecloth), pieced (made from patchwork), or appliquéd; the batting, or wadding; and the backing, which can be plain, or pieced to make a double-sided quilt.

There are various methods of marking fabric for quilting, and many ways to work the stitching. The traditional technique involves taking small even stitches similar to a running stitch, several on the needle at once, with the ideal having the stitches on the back the same length as those on the front. Threads are usually secured with a knot at the end inside the batting. Knots should be taken through to the batting from the back of the work. A tug on the thread should pull the knot through the backing fabric without taking it all the way through to the top. There are also numerous "utility" stitches, from tying to embroidery-type stitches, that have a rough-and-ready look that works well with many traditional patchwork patterns and have the advantage of being quick to work.

Carefully planned and marked quilting can transform a mundane top into a work of great beauty and is well worth the effort. Quilting designs are usually transferred to the quilt top before the piece is layered and basted together. There is a wide selection of markers available, from pencils and chalk to wash-out pens. Test to make sure the marking can be removed before deciding which to use.

**QUILTING TEMPLATES**

1 Make a template for your chosen pattern using lightweight cardboard or special template plastic. The design here is a double cable for use on a border or strippy quilt.

2 Here a dotted stitching line has been marked in pencil using a template made from template plastic.

3 Chalk can be used to mark the design on dark fabrics. All marks should be as light as possible, and markers should be removable. Masking tape can be used to secure the template to the fabric while you mark.

## MARKING STRAIGHT LINES

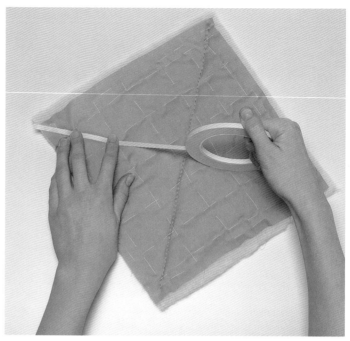

1 Using a ruler and a suitable marker, draw straight lines directly on the fabric.

2 Special low-tack masking tape can also be used to mark straight lines after the piece has been basted. Be careful not to stretch the tape, and do not leave it in place for long periods as it can leave a residue over time.

## MARKING WITH TISSUE PAPER

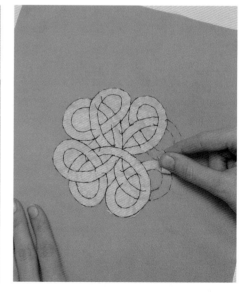

1 Intricate designs can be transferred from a tissue-paper pattern to the fabric. Use small basting stitches and contrasting thread, and position the knots on the right side of the work to make them easier to remove when the time comes.

2 When all the lines have been stitched, run the point of a pin gently along the drawn lines. This will tear the paper along the stitched lines so it can be removed. Take away the outside areas first.

3 Work carefully along the stitched lines of the remaining paper pattern to remove it completely. Pull gently so you don't loosen the basting stitches as you work. The stitching lines are clear and easy to see. You can remove the basting as you work if you wish.

## KNOTS: METHOD 1

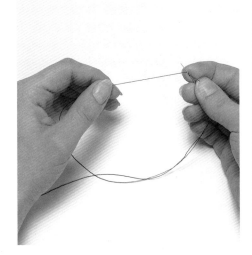

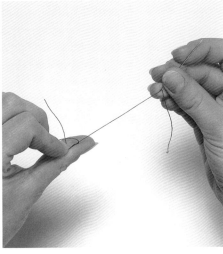

1 Hold the needle between the thumb and index finger with the point upward. Loop the end of the thread around the needle twice, holding it tightly in place.

2 Holding the loops securely, pull down the entire length of the thread to the end, where the knot will catch.

## KNOTS: METHOD 2

1 Hold the needle in your sewing hand so the thread cannot slip out. Loop the loose end of the thread around the first finger of the other hand, and holding it securely, roll the loop off the finger into a knot.

## QUILTING STITCH

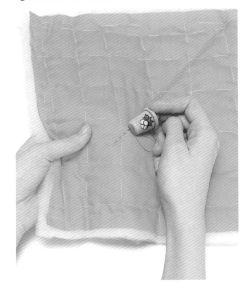

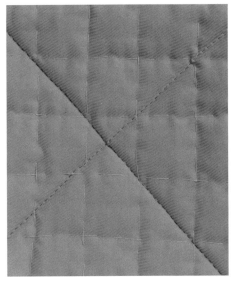

1 Quilting is not an ordinary running stitch. It requires practice to perfect. Insert the needle through all layers and tilt it up, again piercing all the layers. Repeat to make two or three more even stitches, then pull the thread through to the end. If possible, find someone to demonstrate the method to you.

2 Working from the center of the piece outward helps keep the work smooth on the front and the back.

# Utility quilting:

Also known as big-stitch quilting, utility quilting is quick to work and can be found on many older quilts, especially those made in farming areas and African-American communities, where time was precious and it was important to get quilts ready for the bed to provide warmth in the winter.

The stitches shown here are based on embroidery stitches and can be worked using embroidery thread, yarn, or even narrow ribbons as well as quilting thread.

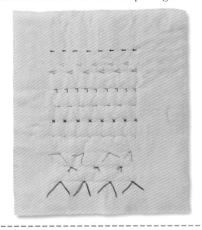

## TRAVELING

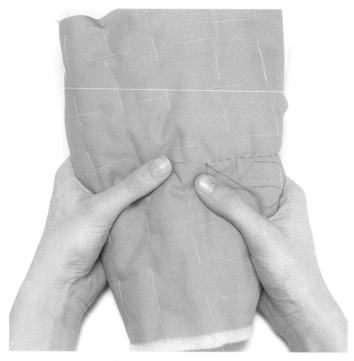

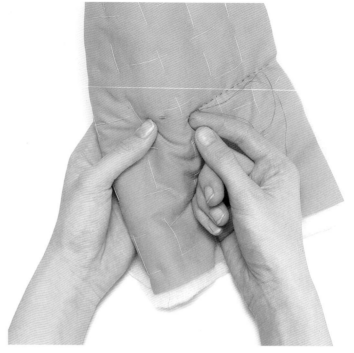

1 To move the thread to an area more than a needle's length away, you can "travel" through the batting. Bring the point of the needle—but only the point—through to the top.

2 Turn the needle over inside the batting so the threaded eye points roughly in the direction you want to go. Push the eye out through the top about a third of the length of the needle.

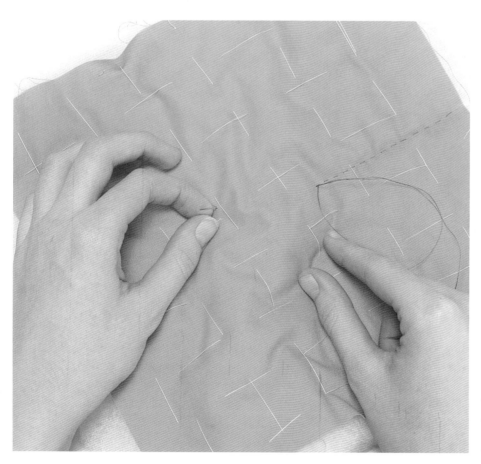

3 Holding the eye carefully, turn the needle again and bring the point through at the start of the new stitching line. Pull the needle and thread all the way out, and begin stitching again. Do not travel more than these two turns of the needle. For greater distances, finish off the thread and start again.

# ways to quilt

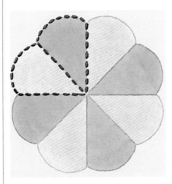

**IN THE DITCH**
Follow the seamlines of a pieced pattern or appliqué shape to secure the layers and create texture. No marking is needed since you are working along previously stitched lines.

**OUTLINE**
Position the stitching ¼ in (5 mm) or more to one side of the seamlines or edges of a motif or pattern. Work inside or outside the lines. Marking can be useful, but may not be essential.

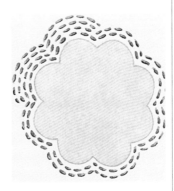

**ECHO**
Repeat the outline around a motif at intervals so the shape of the motif fills the background area around it. Marking will also help to keep the spacing even.

**MOTIF**
Mark the shape to be stitched on the fabric and quilt around the outline. Mark as lightly as possible, but make sure you can see the lines.

**FILLING PATTERNS**
All-over patterns can make a grid or fill in background areas with texture. They can also create a secondary pattern that is not directly related to pieced or applied motifs.

**STIPPLING**
Short stitches placed at random in background areas, called stippling, produce dense areas that flatten the texture or soften the effect.

# Machine quilting

*Until recently, machine quilting was considered inferior to that worked by hand, but the advent of sewing machines designed to cope with the layers and the spreading popularity of long-arm quilting machines have brought the technique into widespread use.*

Well-worked machine quilting is attractive and versatile, aided by the range of machine-embroidery threads that can be used to great effect, and the speed with which quilts can be completed means that machine quilting is here to stay. Most machines have an attachment called a walking foot that helps keep the layers traveling through the machine at the same speed, which keeps the backing layer smooth as you stitch.

Machine quilting is particularly useful for quilts for babies and children, since they will probably be subjected to heavy use and much laundering.

**STRAIGHT LINES**

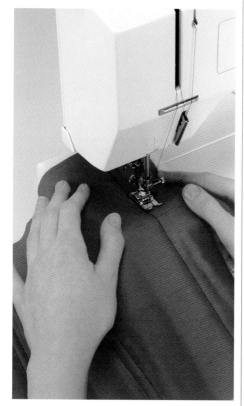

Straight lines can be marked on the fabric and stitched in turn, or you can mark the first line and then use the foot, or a special bar that measures the distance from one line to the next, as a guide to stitching.

**CURVED LINES**

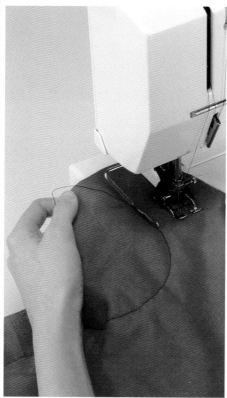

Like straight lines, curved shapes can be marked separately and stitched, or the curve can be followed using the special bar.

**MEANDER STITCH**

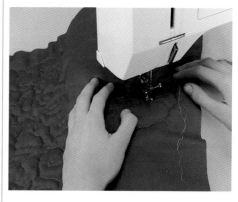

This machine version of stippling gives a closely stitched texture to background areas as it winds its random way around.

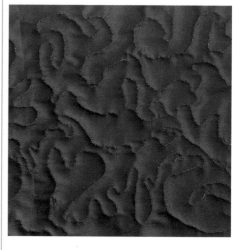

It looks best if the lines are not overstitched, so some planning is needed. Work in small areas in sequence.

**QUILT-AS-YOU-GO**

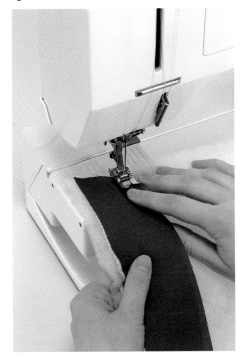

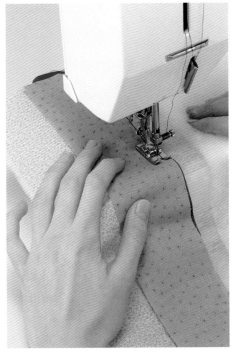

1 Cut a piece of batting about 2 in (5 cm) larger all around than the desired size of the finished piece. Cut out strips of fabric and lay two right sides together along the left-hand edge of the batting. Stitch along the right-hand edge of the strips through all the layers, then open out the top strip.

2 Place a third strip right side down over the second strip and stitch it in place.

**tip:** ROLLING

A large quilt can be difficult to handle under a domestic sewing machine. If you roll up the edges to the area being stitched, the weight will be better distributed and it will be easier to move the piece around. Bicycle clips or special quilting clips can be used to hold the roll in place.

Placing a card table or even an ironing board alongside your sewing table can also make it easier to work on a large quilt—it will extend the size of your sewing area and keep the weight from pulling to the floor as you work.

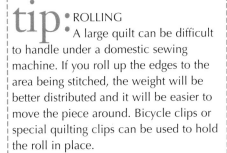

3 Repeat the process to cover the batting, then trim the excess and add backing and borders as desired.

# Embellishment

*Many quilts can be enhanced by the use of decorative embellishment, including beads and buttons, embroidery stitches, and natural found objects like shells or twigs.*

**FRENCH KNOTS**
*One of the most versatile stitches for embellishment, french knots add texture and color, and are useful for making eyes.*

Embellishments are usually added once the basic design has been stitched. Beads, buttons and sequins, lace and net, and decorative embroidery threads and yarns are all available in an astonishing choice of colors, types, and sizes. They can enliven a piece, adding dimension and texture. Yo-yos (Suffolk puffs), cord, rope and string, tassels, and purchased appliqué motifs can all be used, and can be particularly effective on pictorial quilts. Words and images can be embroidered—think of traditional redwork and autograph quilts. The major limiting factor is the maker's imagination. The main danger is the possibility of overworking the piece, so learning to edit the selection of embellishments is important.

**ELONGATED FRENCH KNOTS**
*Elongated french knots have a "tail" extending from the knot and provide a smooth way to attach the bump of the knot to a piece of fabric.*

**BEADS**
*Beads come in all sizes, shapes, and colors. Like french knots, they are good for making eyes, but their usefulness goes much further, since they also add sparkle and texture.*

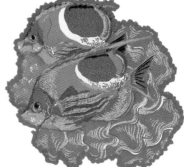

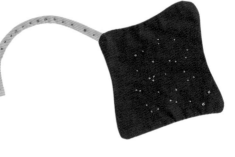

**STRAIGHT STITCH**
*Straight stitches can be worked to highlight details, outline shapes, and for a myriad of other uses as well.*

**SEQUINS**
*Sequins add texture and sparkle. They can be sewn with either side facing up to achieve different effects, and can be secured in place with beads or french knots.*

**SATIN STITCH**
*Machine satin stitch as seen here is a close zigzag stitch that covers raw edges with a clean outline. Worked by hand it can be decorative and versatile.*

**CORDING**
*Laying a decorative thread, cord, braid, or yarn and catching it in place with a hidden sewing stitch is a effective way to add texture and color.*

## stitching by hand

Stitching by hand can be used to piece patchwork, to work appliqué, and to apply embellishment. The stitches shown here are among the most useful to quiltmakers.

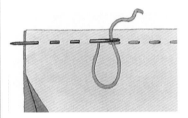

### RUNNING STITCH
Take the needle in and out of the fabric several times, picking up small even stitches. Pull the needle gently through the fabric until the thread is taut, then repeat the sequence to continue stitching.

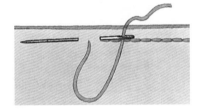

### BACKSTITCH
Bring the needle through to the right side, then insert it back a short distance behind where it first came out. Bring the point out ahead of the resulting stitch the same distance in front of the needle, and repeat the sequence to continue.

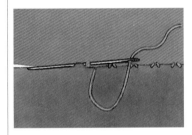

### SLIPSTITCH
Hide the knot in one folded edge and pull the needle and thread through. Pick up a thread or two in the opposite edge and insert the needle back in the first side, next to where the first thread came out. Slide the needle along for a short distance inside the fold, and repeat.

### WHIPSTITCH
Also called overcasting or oversewing, this stitch is worked from left to right. Insert the needle at a slight angle from back to front, picking up one or two threads on each side of the folded edge in each stitch. Pull the thread until it is gently taut, and repeat.

# Finishing

*Once you have completed making a set of patchwork blocks, or worked the
last few stitches of an appliqué design, it is time to finish the quilt.*

There are many questions to be addressed: should
blocks be joined edge to edge, or should there be strips
of fabric, called sashing, between them? How many
borders should there be, and how wide to make them?
Should the blocks be set square, or turned on point?
Should the borders be plain strips, or pieced?

Each quiltmaker sees a finished piece in the mind's
eye, and experience is a good teacher. Look at old
quilts to see what works. Many patchwork patterns
are intended to be set next to each other, creating new
secondary patterns—think of Log Cabin in particular.
Appliqué and pictorial blocks generally look best with
sashing, thin strips of contrasting fabric that set them
off. Sampler quilts—indeed, any design in which the
individual blocks need a separate identy—should be
sashed. Whether you sash or not, you also need to
decide how the blocks should be turned. Blocks can
be set square, with the straight edges parallel to the
sides of the quilt. Many blocks work well, however,
turned on point, with the edges of the blocks at an
angle to the quilt's edges.

Borders act as a frame, enclosing a pattern and
delineating the edge. The width of a border depends
on the overall size of the quilt and the size and
complexity of individual elements. Inner borders
are usually narrower than outer borders, which can
be up to 4 in (10 cm) wide. Pieced borders can give
flair to a simple pattern and finish off an elaborate
one. There are several ways to deal with the corners
of sashing and borders, including stitching straight,
adding contrasting corner squares, and mitering.
And all of these elements will need to be pressed at
each stage. Pressing is essential at each stage of
quiltmaking, but particularly in the early phases,
many seams can simply be pressed with a thumb or
finger, which is known as fingerpressing.

## PRESSING

1 To fingerpress a seam,
press the seam down on the
wrong side with a thumb or
finger to make it lie flat. Take
care not to stretch the fabric.

2 To press with an iron,
set the appropriate
temperature for the fabric
and press down on the wrong
side long enough to make
the seam lie flat. Press—don't
iron. Dragging the iron along
the seam can stretch the
fabric out of shape.

## SASHING

1 Sashing usually runs both
horizontally and vertically.
Cut sashing strips to the
desired width plus seams.

2 Join a short strip to one
side of the block, then
join the next block to the
other edge of the strip. Repeat
to make rows of sashed blocks
as required and press the
seams to one side.

3 Stitch a long strip to one
row of sashed blocks, then
join the next row to the other
long edge of the strip. Repeat
to join the rows to assemble
the quilt top. Press the seams.

## STRAIGHT BORDERS

1 To make top-and-tail borders, cut border strips to the desired width plus seams and add them to opposite sides of the quilt in sequence. Here the short edges—top and bottom—have been sewn first, followed by the long side edges.

2 To make a continuous border, start about 4 in (10 cm) down from the right-hand corner of the quilt. Apply the first strip, but leave enough length at the top of the strip to overhang the top edge plus the width of the border strip. Add the second, third, and fourth strips working clockwise around the quilt. To finish the first strip, turn the quilt and stitch the unsewn end by continuing the seamline where you began, catching in the end of the fourth strip (see also Steps 2 and 4 of Corner Squares, right).

## CORNER SQUARES

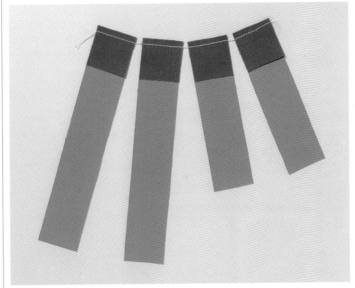

1 To incorporate corner squares into sashing or borders, cut the strips, and cut contrasting squares the same width. Stitch a square to one end of each strip and press the seams to one side. These strips have been chain-pieced (see page 42).

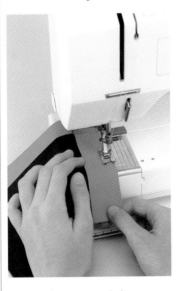

3 Working around the sides clockwise, add the remaining strips, placing the next corner square at the end of the strip just sewn.

4 When you get back to the beginning, continue the initial seam to incorporate the first corner square.

2 Line up the first strip so that the corner square overhangs the top edge of the piece being bound or sashed. Mark the beginning of the seam about 4 in (10 cm) below the top of the quilt or block and start stitching there.

5 Press the seams. Note that here the seams are pressed toward the outside edge of the quilt as required by the construction, not toward the darker fabric.

**SETTING BLOCKS**

1 To set blocks square, add sashing in both directions, or set the blocks edge to edge. Sashing has been used on this quilt to emphasize the individual design of each block.

2 To set blocks on point, turn each block 90 degrees so that the corners point to the sides of the quilt. On this quilt, sashing and corner squares were added to the blocks and made into rows, with filling triangles added at the ends before the blocks were joined.

## MITERED CORNER

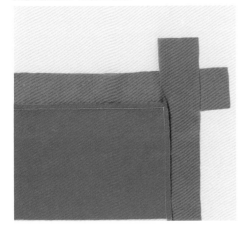  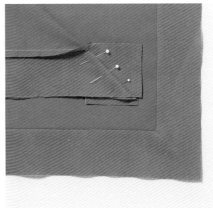

1 Mitered corners meet at a 45-degree angle and must be precise. Cut strips longer than the edge of the quilt plus borders. Measure ¼ in (5 mm) in from each corner and starting and finishing at the marked point, apply the strips.

2 Fold back each strip to a 45-degree angle and press to mark the fold. Working from the right side, pin along the fold to hold the seam in place.

3 Turn the corner to the wrong side and re-pin with the pins at right angles to the fold. Make sure the two foldlines match precisely on both sides and stitch from the inner corner toward the edge. Trim the ends.

4 Miters give a smooth professional finish.

## PIECED BORDERS

Chevrons          Flying geese          Squares          Two-tone rectangles          Prairie points

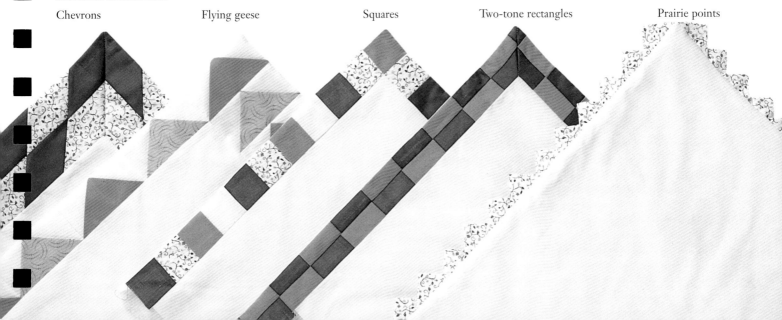

## JOINING PLAIN AND PIECED UNITS

1 Many patterns involve joining a plain block to a pieced unit. The triangle square here was made first and must be the same size as the plain block.

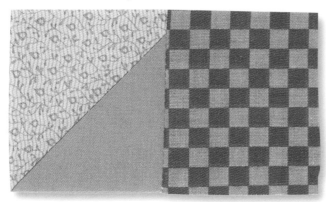

2 When these two units are joined, the corner of the pieced block is caught in the seam. The distance between the raw edge and the now-visible corner of the triangle must measure ¼ in (5 mm).

3 When two of these units are combined to make a four-patch block, the seam allowance becomes hidden and the four corners meet precisely in the middle.

---

## tip: UNPICKING SEAMS

Sometimes it becomes necessary to unpick, or rip out, a stitched seam. Mistakes happen and can often be rescued, and various construction methods involve sewing seams that are then opened up to manipulate the units before being sewn again.

To avoid damaging the fabric, always use a seam ripper instead of scissors. Clean away bits of thread before restitching—pointed tweezers can be handy for this.

### RIPPING ON ONE SIDE

1 Holding the seam taut, insert the point of the seam ripper into every third or fourth stitch and break the thread.

2 Hold the bottom strip and pull the top strip gently to separate the stitches.

Do not use this method on bias seams.

### UNPICKING DOWN THE MIDDLE

1 Hold the seam open and insert the seam ripper between the strips and break the thread. Gently pull the seam apart and repeat to the end.

# Quilting Bs

*There are five "B" words in quilting, all techniques that are involved in finishing a piece. The first four: batting, backing, bagging, and basting are all stages between finishing a top and starting the quilting. The fifth, binding, is the welcome final task.*

**BATTING**
80 % polyester
20 % cotton

Polyester
needlepunch

Cotton

Dark polyester

2 oz (60 g) polyester

4 oz (125 g) polyester

Batting, or wadding, is the material used as the middle layer in a quilt, as well as the word used to define the process of padding the piece. Its original purpose was to provide warmth as well as softness, and old quilts can be found batted with worn blankets or even older quilts, combed wool or cotton fibers, or layers of fabric. Modern batting is made from polyester, cotton, or a poly/cotton blend sold by the yard from rolls, or packaged cut into standard quilt sizes. Wool and silk versions are also available, usually by special order. Most batting is white, but a dark gray version can also be found. Because batting draws up when it is quilted, it should always be cut slightly larger than the size of the quilt top.

Backing is both the fabric used on the underside of a quilt and its application when the quilt is layered. It should match or coordinate with the quilt top and be suitable for quilting. Cotton sheeting sold in extra-wide widths is ideal, or lengths of appropriate weight can be joined to make up the required width.

Bagging, or bagging out, is a method of batting, backing, and finishing the edges of a quilt in a single operation. The layers are placed with the quilt top and backing right sides together on the batting. All three layers are stitched together around all four sides, leaving a gap in the center of the bottom edge for turning right side out.

Basting is loose temporary stitching that holds the layers in place as you quilt. Layers can also be "basted" with safety pins at regular intervals or with a washable, repositionable spray-on fabric adhesive. Bagged quilts cannot be basted until after they have been bagged, but quilts that are to be bound are layered and basted to keep them smooth, then quilted, before the binding is applied.

Binding the edges of a quilt means that the final stage has been reached. There are several methods of binding, each of which has its advantages. Single binding is made from long strips that have the edges folded to the middle to create a fold along which to stitch. It creates a single layer of binding along the edge and can be purchased precut and folded, or you can make your own. Double binding is folded lengthwise in the middle and handled like single binding. Its double strength makes it ideal for quilts that will be laundered frequently. The edge-to-middle technique is often found on antique quilts. It provides a strong clean edge. Back-to-front (or front-to-back) binding makes a neat single layer of binding and ties the sides of the quilt together visually. The backing is larger all around than the quilt top and batting, and the edges of the backing fabric are folded to the front. The method you choose will depend on personal preference, the design of the quilt itself, and the amount of use the quilt will receive.

## BACKING

Backing should not have a seam down the middle of the piece. If you must join fabrics to make a piece large enough to back the quilt, place a full width of backing fabric in the center and add a narrower piece on each side.

## BASTING DIRECTION

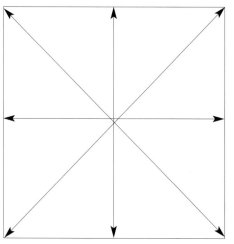

Baste from the center outward, vertically, horizontally, and diagonally, spacing the rows about 4 in (10 cm) apart.

## STITCHED BASTING

Sandwich the quilt layers together and smooth out the creases. Use large slanted running stitches to sew through all layers. Use an old teaspoon to press down and lift the point of the needle where it emerges.

## PIN BASTING

Sandwich the layers and smooth out the creases. Insert rustproof safety pins at regular intervals.

## BAGGING

1 Lay the batting flat and place the quilt top right side up on it. Place the backing fabric right side down on the quilt top and smooth all the wrinkles. Pin and stitch around the outside edges, leaving a 5–10 in (12–25 cm) opening, depending on the size of the quilt, for turning it right side out.

2 Cut away any excess batting and backing fabric, grading the seams if necessary, and trim the corners to reduce bulk. Turn the quilt right side out through the opening and turn the raw edges to the inside. Press them gently, pin, and slipstitch to close the opening.

tip: Sometimes, such as when you reach a corner when bagging out a quilt, you need to change sewing direction without breaking the thread. To keep the thread continuous, you can raise the presser foot without lifting the needle and turn the work to a different direction.

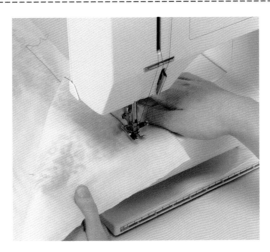

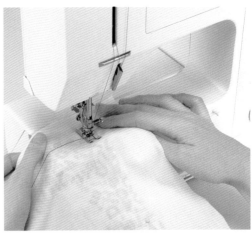

1 When you reach a corner, stop the machine a seam width from the perpendicular edge, leaving the needle in the fabric. Lift the presser foot and turn the work at a right angle to the seam you have just stitched.

2 With the needle still in the fabric, lower the presser foot and continue stitching along the next seamline. This method is the same for all machine sewing, including machine quilting.

## SINGLE BINDING

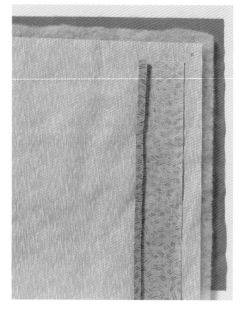

1 Cut strips of binding 1–2 in (2.5–5 cm) wide and press a ¼ in (5 mm) fold along one long edge. Mark a point ¼ in (5 mm) from each edge on the right side in each corner of the quilt top.

2 Place the binding right side down on the quilt top, aligning the unpressed long edge of the binding with the edge of the quilt layers. Stitch the edge, starting and finishing at the corner marks.

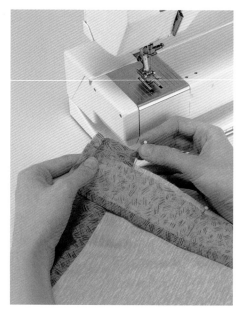

3 Open out the stitched strip and pin a new strip to the adjacent edge, starting again at the corner mark. Stitch along this edge as before, making sure you do not catch the first strip in the new stitching line. Repeat to bind all edges.

4 Turn the folded edge of the binding to the quilt back to cover the raw edges, pinning as you work.

5 When you reach a corner, fold the cut edge at the end of each strip of binding to the inside and square off the corner. To finish, pin and slipstitch around all the edges

6 The top quilt is bound with single binding, while the lower one is double bound (see opposite).

## DOUBLE BINDING

1 Cut strips twice as wide as the finished binding plus ½ in (10 mm) seam allowances. Fold in half lengthwise, wrong sides together, and press flat.

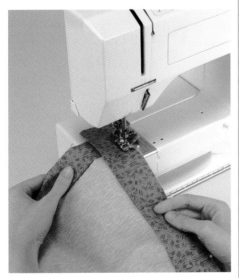

2 Mark, pin, and sew as for Single Binding, stitching along the double-thickness raw edges of the binding. Turn the folded edge to the back, and pin and slipstitch in place.

## EDGE-TO-MIDDLE BINDING

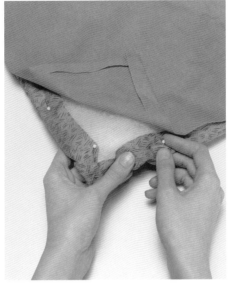

1 Cut the batting smaller all around than the squared-up backing, and make sure the edges of the quilt top are even all around. Turn under the edges of the quilt top and pin or baste them in place. Fold the edges of the backing fabric over the batting and pin through all the layers. Remove pins used on the back.

## BACK-TO-FRONT BINDING

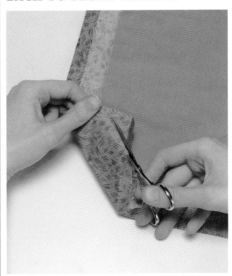

1 Trim the batting to the same size as the quilt top and square up the edges of the backing, making them the desired width of the binding plus seam allowances. Turn ¼ in (5 mm) to the wrong side on all edges of the backing and press the fold. Fold a miter at each corner and trim the seam allowance.

2 Secure the edges with a double row of topstitching. Work the first row ¼ in (5 mm) from the finished edge, with the second row ¼ in (5 mm) inside the first, turning corners sharply (see box, page 65).

2 Fold the pressed edges of the backing to the front of the quilt and pin them in place. Stitch by hand or by machine along all sides, and slipstitch the miters to finish. This binding can be done the other way around, folding the front to the back instead if you wish.

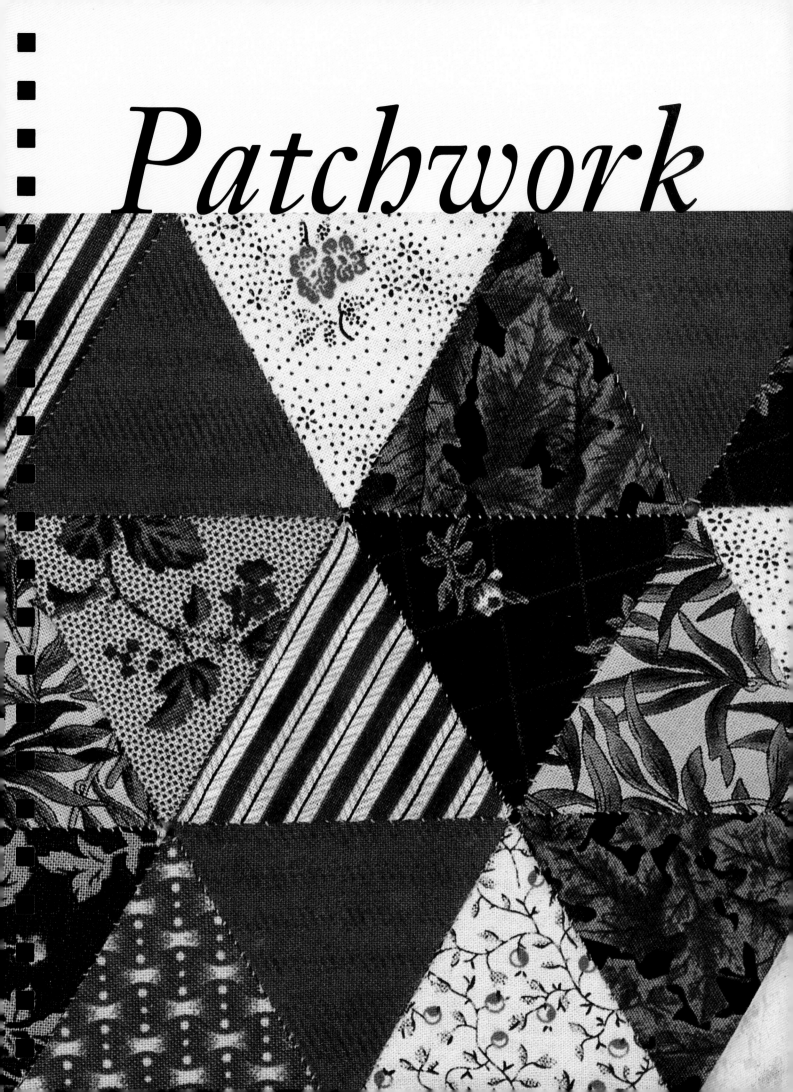

# CHAPTER 3

# Patchwork

# Strips: Rail Fence

STRIPS ARE USED TO MAKE A VARIETY of patchwork patterns. They are easy to cut, and their versatility makes them a popular starting point for many patchwork blocks. Strip patterns, especially Log Cabin and the simple Rail Fence block shown here, are widely used to teach beginners, but there are numerous more complex strip blocks, such as Roman Stripe in which one diagonal half of a square is made from strips, that appeal to quilters at all levels.

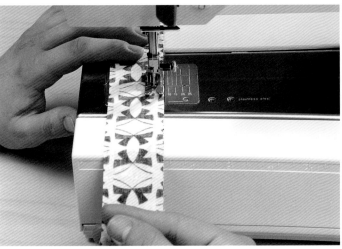

1 Cut 1½ in (4 cm) strips from all three fabrics—light, medium, and dark.

2 Sew strips together. We have arranged ours in a dark, light, medium order. Press the seams to one side, in this case, away from the light strip in the middle. The pieced strip measures 3½ in (9 cm).

3 Cut the strips into 3½ in (9 cm) squares. You will need 16 squares to make the block.

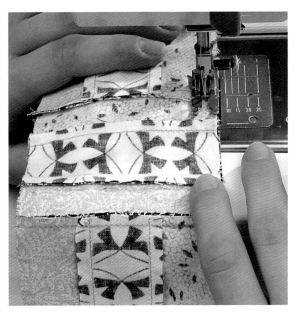

4 Sew squares with the strips alternating vertically, then horizontally, into four rows of four units each. Make sure the order of the dark/light/medium values is consistent, and begin two rows with a square turned vertically and two with the first square turned horizontally. Press the seams to one side.

5 Join the rows, again so that the first square in each row alternates with the one in the next row. Press the seams to one side to complete the block, or expand the concept to create an entire quilt.

# Nine-patch: Grecian block

BLOCK PATCHWORK IS A FAVORITE way of putting together a quilt. Each block is made up of nine units. The simplest of these units are squares of equal size, but countless variations exist in which the squares are made of smaller squares, or triangles, or rectangular strips. This block contains all three: the central unit is a square of medium value, the corners are triangle squares of light and dark values, and the middle units are strips, also of light and dark, that form rectangles in the block.

**note:** Double nine-patch blocks are composed of units that are divided into smaller Nine-patch units. There are also blocks that contain four Nine-patch units, and others with nine Four-patch units. Experimenting with color, value, and arrangement of units is always fun and rewarding ... you may find you have invented an entirely new block.

1 Cut 2½ in (6 cm) strips from the light and the dark fabrics.

2 Cut two 4⅞ in (12.5 cm) squares from the light and two from the dark fabrics. Cut one 4½ in (11.5 cm) square from the medium fabric.

3 Sew the strips lengthwise, right sides together. (Inset) Press the seam to the dark side.

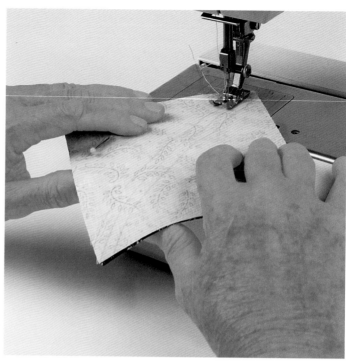

4 Cut four squares measuring 4½ in (11.5 cm) from the joined strip and set them aside.

5 Make four triangles squares from the larger 4⅞ in (12.5 cm) squares (see page 43).

6 Cut them apart across the diagonal. (Inset) Press the seams to the dark side.

7 Join the nine units. First, make three rows of units: two identical rows comprising two corner (triangle) blocks and one middle (rectangle) block, bearing in mind that the light triangles are at the ends of the strips and the dark rectangles are on the edge that will become the outside edges of the block.

Then make the central row, positioning the two remaining rectangle units with the light strips adjacent to the plain central square.

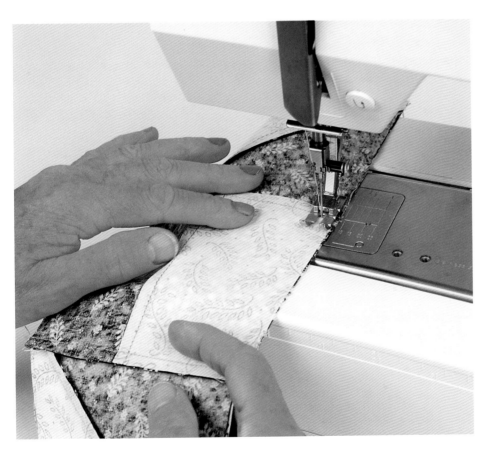

8 Join the three rows in order to complete the block, with the light rectangle strips adjacent to the central square.

# Four-patch variation: Star

THERE ARE NUMEROUS STAR PATTERNS, but few are as simple to construct as this variation of a four-patch block that creates an eight-point star using only squares and triangle squares. This block can be made as a double four-patch (see NOTE, below right), but our construction method eliminates several seams and makes the blocks easier to quilt.

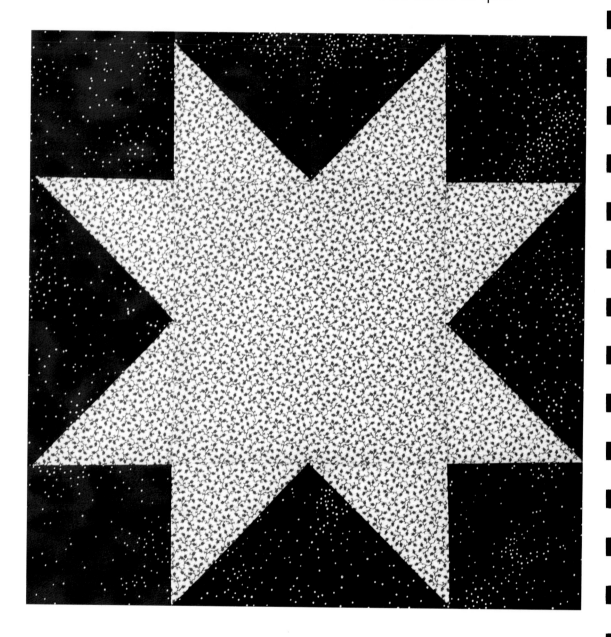

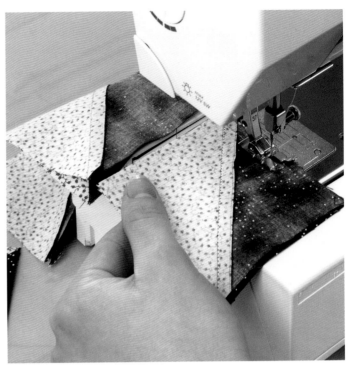

1 Making this design our way eliminates seams in the central square, which looks neater and gives a good seamless area for quilting (see NOTE below).

Cut a 6½ in (16.5 cm) square (ours is red and white) for the center of the star. Cut strips of each fabric 3⅞ in (10 cm) wide.

2 Make eight triangle squares as shown on page 43 and cut them apart.

3 Join two triangle squares along blue edges as shown to make four pairs of units. These form the points of the star. Press the seams to one side

4 Join two of the pairs of "points" to opposite sides of the center square. Make sure they are stitched so that the points are not blunted. Press the seams toward the center square.

5 Cut four 3½ in (9 cm) squares from the blue background fabric. Join one square to each end of the two remaining sets of "points" and press the seams toward the blue squares.

note: If you wish to make the star as a double four-patch block, cut four 3½ in (9 cm) squares of the red-and-white fabric and join them into a square for the center area. Then proceed from Step 2 above.

6 Sew one strip to each side of the center section and press the seams toward the center.

# Representational: Basket block

THIS CAKESTAND BLOCK IS A SIMPLE basket pattern. Like most representational blocks, it usually works best with sashing to set it off from other blocks in a quilt, and it looks wonderful set "on point," in which case setting triangles can be placed on each side instead of sashing strips.

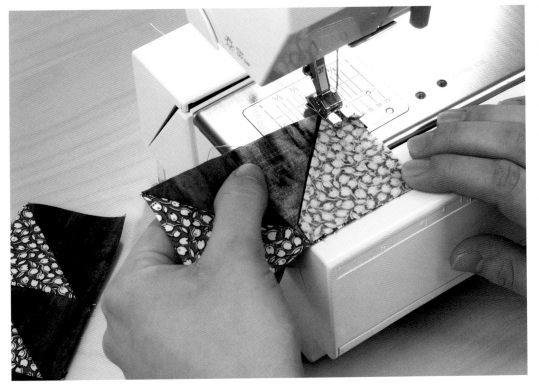

1 The basket handle and foot are made from triangle squares. Cut 2⅞ in (7 cm) strips from the blue and the red tulip print fabrics and make eight triangle squares (see page 43). Cut them apart and press the seams to one side, then trim off the tails.

Join three triangle squares to make a strip, then join three more with the blue triangles running in the opposite direction to make another strip. The remaining two squares will be used later.

2 You also need one large triangle of blue and one of red tulip fabric to make the center of the block. The easiest way to cut these accurately is to cut a 7 in (18 cm) square from each fabric and cut it in half along one diagonal. Join the two triangles along the diagonal and press the seam to one side. The other half of each square can go in your scrap basket.

3 Add one strip of small triangle squares to one red side of the large triangle square. Make sure the bases of the blue triangles are against the red fabric. Mark each point of the triangle with a pin to make sure you don't blunt them when you stitch.

4 Cut one 2½ in (6 cm) square from the blue fabric. Add it to the end of the unsewn strip of small triangle squares. Then sew the strip to the other red side of the large triangle square.

5 Cut seven 2½ in (6 cm) squares from the red tulip fabric. Sew three together to make a strip and repeat to make another strip.

Sew one of the remaining small red and blue triangle squares to the end of each strip, making sure that the blue triangles point in opposite directions. Sew the seventh red square to the end of one strip next to the triangle square.

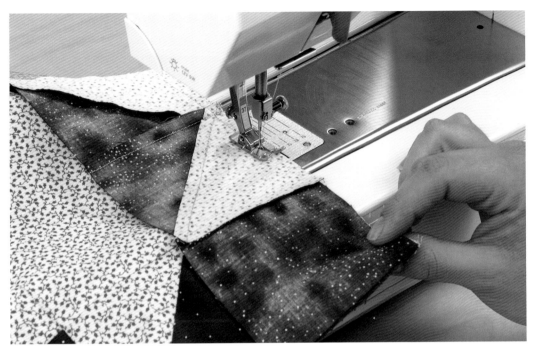

6 Add these strips to the blue edges of the block, stitching the shorter one first, then the longer one to make the base of the basket.

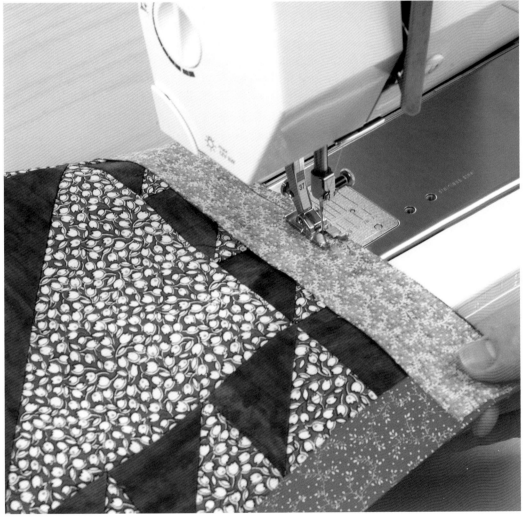

7 Cut 1½-in (4 cm) -wide strips from the bright red mini-print fabric and add them to the edges of the block to frame it.

tip: Placing a pin at the point of each triangle being sewn helps you make sure you don't stitch through the point and cut it off.

# Curves: Drunkard's Path

CURVED SEAMS ARE TRICKIER to sew than straight ones, but with careful cutting and pinning they are easy to stitch, and they create a sense of fluid movement that can never be achieved using straight lines. Curved patterns can be stitched by hand or machine.

1 Cut a 4½ in (11 cm) strip from the dark fabric—ours is red. Cut a 3½ in (9 cm) strip from the light fabric—ours has a white background. Trace the templates on pags 155 and transfer them to cardboard or template plastic. You need four pieces: two with seam allowances and two without.

2 The block is a simple nine-patch, so you will need nine units, each made of a light and a dark piece. If you fold the strips cut in Step 1 with right sides together, you can transfer the template to one half and cut two pieces at a time, but since you need nine pieces, you will need to cut one individually.

Using the templates with seam allowances, transfer the smaller shape to the 3½ in (9 cm) strip and the larger shape to the 4½ in (11 cm) strip. These marks are the cutting lines. Pin the strips together inside the cutting lines.

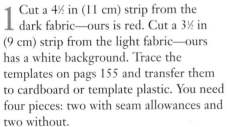

3 Using scissors, cut out the shapes. You will need nine of each for one block.

tip: Because curved seams are always cut on the cross grain, they are highly vulnerable to stretching. Handle the pieces as little as possible and always cut notches to make matching the concave and convex curves easier.

4 Using the templates without seam allowances, mark the seamline on the wrong side of each piece, paying special attention to the notches. You may need to mark only the curved edges.

5 Place a larger shape right side up in front of you. Position a smaller shape, right sides together, on the larger shape and pin them together. Match the center notches, then the corners, then pin the intermediate notches. Add more pins if necessary.

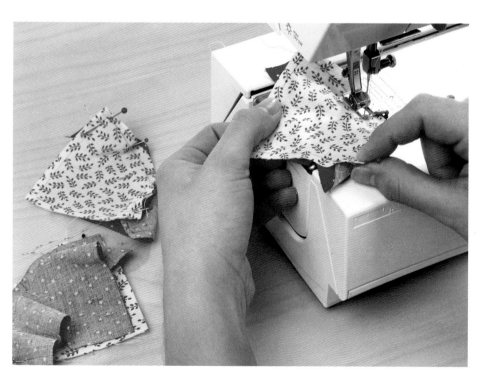

7 Press the seams on the wrong side of the piece toward the larger piece. If you have cut and stitched accurately, there is no need to clip the curves.

6 Using a ¼ in (5 mm) foot on the machine, stitch along the curved edges of each piece using the marked seamlines to guide you. Remove pins as you work. You can chain-piece for speed.

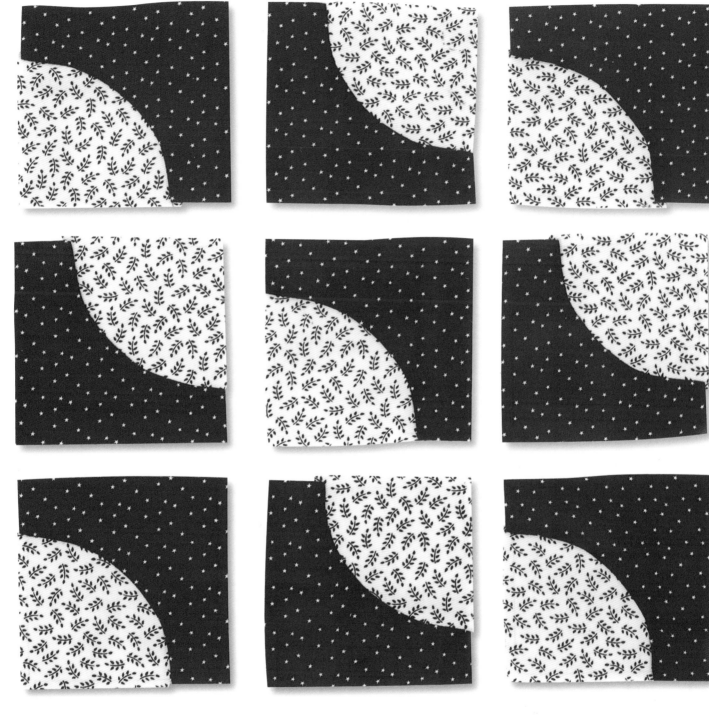

8 Lay out the completed units to create three rows of three. The blocks are in fact all combined in the same order, but the middle row is turned 180 degrees to create the Drunkard's Path pattern.

Stitch the blocks together in rows and press the seams of each row in opposite directions. Join the rows together.

note: There are many variations for the Drunkard's Path pattern, such as Snake in the Hollow, Chain Link, Love Ring, and Falling Timbers.

# Seminole band

SEMINOLE PATCHWORK IS CREATED when strips of fabric are joined lengthwise and cut into units that are then stitched into alternate configurations. Many of the most effective patterns are cut at an angle and offset when they are restitched. The bands that are created can be used to decorate garments and home furnishings, and make wonderful pieced borders for quilts. The Seminole technique can also be used to create Bargello patterns, in which the fabrics are stepped up and down the row.

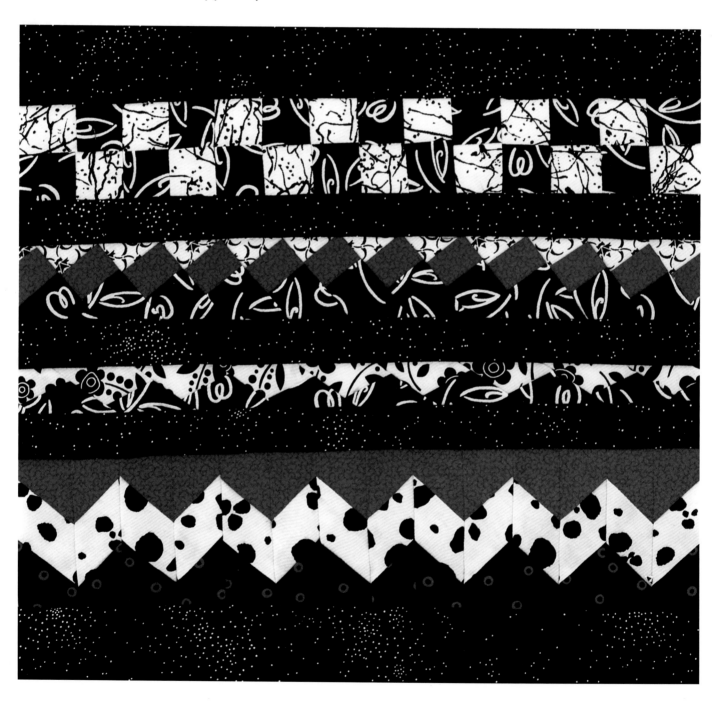

## ALTERNATING STRIPS

1A Perhaps the simplest Seminole design is alternating squares. Cut strips 1½ in (4 cm) wide in two highly contrasting colors. Stitch them together lengthwise and press the seam toward the darker fabric. Cut the strip widthwise into 1½ in (4 cm) wide units.

1B Alternate the units to make a checkerboard strip. The units can be chain-pieced in pairs and the pairs then joined. Press the seams carefully.

## THREE-COLOR CHEVRON

2A Cut the top strip 1½ in (4 cm), the middle strip 1¼ in (3.5 cm), the bottom strip 2 in (5 cm) and stitch them together lengthwise. If you reverse the direction in which you sew the first seam to join on the third strip, you will eliminate the bowing that can occur when stitching long seams, which will create mismatched seams in the next step. Press the completed strip.

2B Cut the strip widthwise to make thirteen 1½ in (4 cm) wide units and join them together by aligning the top of the middle color on one unit with the bottom of the middle color on the next unit. You can chain piece them in pairs and then join the pairs.

2C When all the units have been joined, press the strip and trim the points that now make the top and bottom edges of the strip to level it off.

**TWO-COLOR ZIGZAG**

3A Stitched strips can also be cut at an angle and joined to make zigzag patterns. Cut two contrasting strips, each 1¾ in (4.5 cm) wide, and join them. Press the seam toward the darker fabric. Measure a 60-degree angle with your rotary ruler and cut the end of the strip at the correct angle. Then cut ten 1½ in (4 cm) wide units at the same angle.

tip: You can choose any angle on the rotary ruler, but it is crucial to make sure you cut the same angle on each piece.

3B Join the units in pairs, staggering the middle seam by ½ in (1 cm) each time. The raw edges of each unit are cut along a partial bias and can be stretched out of shape easily, so work carefully. Join the pairs to make a zigzag strip and press.

3C Trim the points of the top and bottom edges of the strip level as in Step 2c.

**THREE-COLOR**

4A Angled strips can also be cut in opposite directions to make zigzag patterns. Cut three contrasting strips, each 1½ in (4 cm) wide. Stitch the strips together as in Step 2a. Cut the long strip in half widthwise and press the seams on one half toward the center and on the other half toward the outside edges. This means that the seam allowances will "nest" next to each other when you join them. Lay the two strips on the cutting mat, right sides together, and measure a 45-degree angle at one end of each piece in opposite directions. Cut seven units in each direction.

> note: Press the seams of each unit in opposite directions before stitching them together. The seams will lie against each other and create a smooth match and reducing bulkiness.

4B Join the units in opposite pairs, aligning the seams of each piece. Then join the pairs to create a chevron strip. Press. Remember that the raw edges are on the bias and will stretch easily if not handled with extreme care.

4C Trim the points at the top and bottom of the strip level as in Step 2c.

# Crazy patchwork

CRAZY PATCHWORK, AND ITS COUSIN string piecing, are wonderful related techniques for using up scraps from other projects. Crazy patchwork was beloved by Victorian needlewomen, and among the finest late nineteenth-century quilts are examples made this way from fine fabrics such as silk and velvet left over from dressmaking projects and beautifully decorated with embroidery and small appliqués. String piecing is the "poor relation," found primarily on historical quilts among examples made in African-American homes from whatever size, type, or shape of scrap came to hand. Often these were long "strings" of fabric cut off the grain and also left over from dressmaking or home sewing, often done for paying customers. In spite of their humble beginnings, quilts made from the technique are usually lively and inventive, combining a variety of patterns as well as types of fabric, from cotton and wool to corduroy, denim, and upholstery.

**BAT THE MAT**
*Add a layer of batting for extra protection if you wish, and bind according to your preferred method. We have used the back-to-front technique (see page 67).*

# note:
The foundation can be muslin (calico) or a similar fabric if you are making a quilt or throw, but we have used craft felt to assemble this placemat, which gives it more stability and provides more protection for the table. Such mats are quick to make, you can use the same fabrics in different configurations to create a set to match your decor, and they are great to give as gifts.

You can plan the layout in advance, or you can simply work with random pieces from your scrap basket, but make sure you have a variety of color values.

1 Cut a foundation of felt—ours measures 9 x 12 in (23 x 30 cm). Gather a selection of scraps and press them. Try to choose a variety of color values: light, medium, and dark—and have a selection of sizes and shapes available.

2 Lay the first piece of fabric right side up in the center of the foundation. Place the next piece right side down on it, aligning the raw edges, and stitch it in place through all three layers using a ¼ in (5 mm) seam. Flip Piece 2 to the right side and fingerpress the seam.

3 Choose another piece of fabric and place it right side down along one edge of Pieces 1 and 2. Work clockwise around the foundation. If the chosen piece does not fit exactly, trim away any excess fabric before you flip the new piece to the right side. Trim off thread ends before you continue.

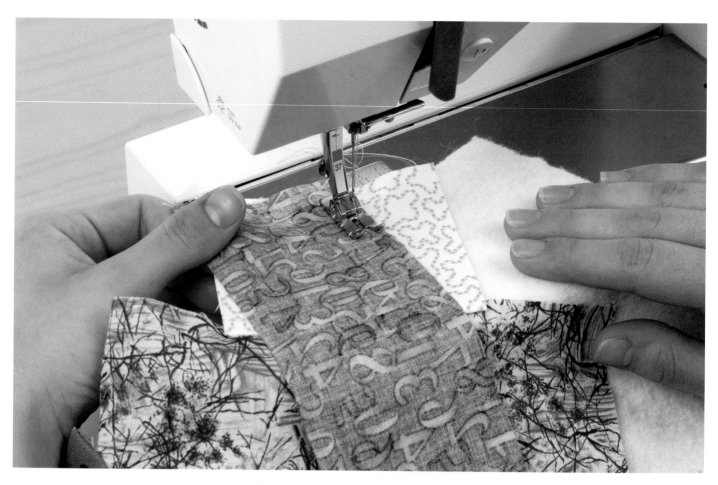

4 Repeat Step 2 with the fourth piece of fabric and continue working around the foundation, adding each piece in turn, trimming, and clipping thread ends. If the seams run parallel, the desired randomness is not so effective, so make sure that all the seams run in different directions.

5 Each piece should be pressed after it is stitched. This wooden device is designed to be used for firm fingerpressing, or you can use an iron.

6 Try to avoid shapes that need to be set in. If possible, plan one piece ahead. Here we can add a small scrap to cover the bottom edge, stitching one edge in place by machine and sewing the other with the seam allowance turned under by hand.

We felt that the upper left-hand piece was too large to make a balanced design, so we added a final yellow triangle in that corner.

7 When the last piece has been stitched, turned, and trimmed, lay the completed mat wrong side up on a cutting mat. Trim the excess fabric around the edges and square up the shape before backing and binding the work.

# Pictorial: Landscape

SUBJECTS FOR PICTORIAL QUILTS include portraits of people and animals, scenery, and forms from nature, and choosing a theme is a personal decision. Landscapes, both highly representational and fairly abstract, are widely made, and provide quilters at all levels of skill with the opportunity to stretch their imaginations and technical ability.

Pictorial work is also a popular medium for art quilters. The abstract landscape shown here is actually quite simple in its concept, and its effectiveness relies on both the superb fabric choices and the technical skill of the designer, Barbara Ritchey.

1 Trace the pattern on pages 156–157 and enlarge it to the desired size. Ours measures 15 x 18 in (38 x 46 cm). Make a paper pattern and cut it apart. Cut out the fabric pieces, adding a seam allowance all around. The strips at the bottom measure 19 in (48 cm) long. The darker narrow strip is 1½ in (4 cm) wide, the wider strip is 2¾ in (7 cm) wide. Cut out batting and backing fabric measuring 17 x 20 in (43 x 51 cm) and baste them together with the batting face up on the wrong side of the backing.

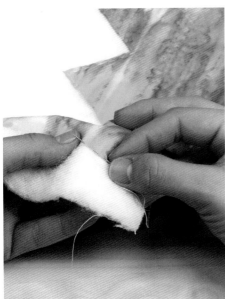

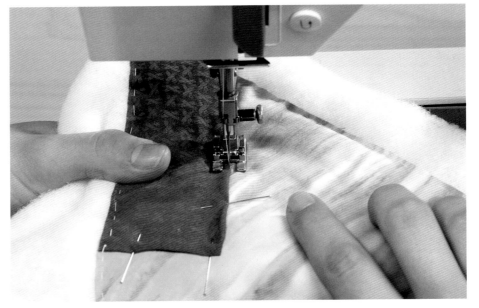

2 Position the first piece of the design fabric—the sky—right side up on the two layers. Baste around all edges to secure the sky piece.

3 The pieces must be added in order. To add pieces 2 and 3, align the bottom and side raw edges, which will be covered in their turn, with the first piece and baste as before. Turn under the allowance on the top edges that cover the raw edges of the sky piece and press lightly, then pin

them in place. Using a machine blindstitch, sew these edges in position, removing the pins as you work. If your machine does not have this function, you can use a very narrow zigzag stitch, but the finished effect will be slightly different. You can also slipstitch by hand.

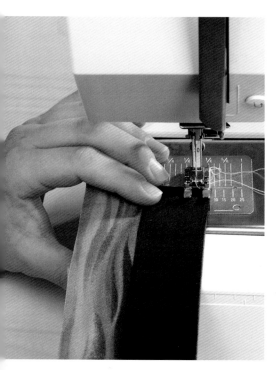

4 Repeat Step 3 to add the fourth piece. (Inset) Continue adding Pieces 5 and 6 in the same way to complete the "mountain range".

5 Stitch the two strips right sides together and press the seam open.

6 Stitch the joined strips to the bottom of the mountain range, right sides together, to hide the seam allowance.

7 Press the strips to the right side and baste around the raw side edges and bottom. Trim and bind the edges (see pages 66–67). The finished hanging is shown on page 94.

note: Creating a full-size pattern for pictorial work will make it easier to see the overall impact of the design and to assess fabric requirements.

# English paper piecing: Mosaic triangles

ENGLISH PAPER PIECING IS THE technique by which small irregular shapes, such as triangles, diamonds, and hexagons in particular, were traditionally joined to make patchwork designs. Widely practiced in Britain in the nineteenth century, it provides an accurate method for working with these shapes using hand sewing. Using freezer paper instead of traditional heavy paper like stationery for the backings makes the task quicker to work.

1 Trace the triangle shape on page 154 on template plastic or stiff cardboard. This will be the finished size of the triangles. Use it to draw the required number of shapes on the matte side of freezer paper (see Note below).

2 Cut out the freezer paper shapes using paper scissors. You can cut a few at a time, or cut them all at once and keep them in a bag or box. Iron them to the wrong side of the chosen fabrics, leaving room around each triangle for a seam allowance—we suggest at least ½ in (1 cm) between.

3 Cut out the fabric shapes, leaving a ¼ in (5 mm) seam allowance on all sides.

4 Turn the seam allowance to the wrong side over the edges of the paper and baste in place around all sides.

6 Remove the basting and the papers and back the mat. We have used felt, applied with fusible web.

5 Slipstitch triangles together, using a betweens needle and thread to blend. We have begun by combining six triangles into hexagon shapes that can then be joined, but you can also sew triangles together in strips.

note: Freezer paper can be purchased from quilt stores, but it is also available in the household section of most supermarkets. It has a matte, paper side that can be drawn on, and a shiny side that clings to fabric when it is ironed in place, but which can easily be removed.

# Foundation piecing: Kite block

ALSO KNOWN AS PAPER PIECING, this method is widely used to make pictorial blocks. Shapes are joined by stitching pieces together on the wrong side of a paper or pellon (vilene ) pattern which is then removed when the block is finished. Many designs can be adapted to create foundation patterns.

1 Copy the full-size patterns for the kite design on pages 158–159, making sure you copy the numbers as well. Pattern A is the front of the design, Patterns B and C are the back. This method is worked from the back and Patterns B and C are the ones on which you stitch. You need to see through it to check the seamlines before you stitch, so you need to copy them on tracing paper or parchment paper. Set them aside while you cut out the fabric pieces.

Cut the pieces of Pattern A apart and pin each one to the right side of its fabric. You can use scraps, and because any excess fabric is trimmed after each seam is stitched, you can cut them out roughly.

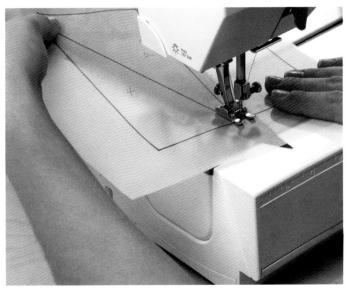

2 Cut apart Patterns B and C. Place Pattern B face down and position Piece 1 right side up so that it covers the corresponding area on the pattern. You can check this by holding the pattern up to the light to make sure the fabric covers all the relevant stitching lines and that there is at least ¼ in (5 mm) seam allowance on all sides. Place Piece 2 right side together with Piece 1.

3 Put an open appliqué foot on your sewing machine and set the stitch length for a very short stitch—we've used 1.5. This makes it easier to remove the paper when the block is completed.

With Pattern B face up and the two fabric pieces underneath, stitch along the seamline that joins the two pieces.

tip: It is relatively straightforward to create your own patterns for foundation piecing. Just be sure to number the pieces carefully.

4 Turn the work with the fabric on top. Open the pieces and press along the seam.

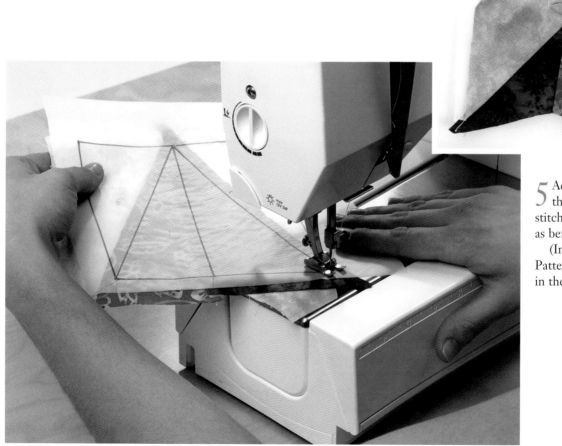

5 Add Pieces 3 and 4 in the same way, positioning, stitching, and opening as before.
   (Inset) Pieces 5–8 on Pattern C are put together in the same way.

6 The two halves of the kite are joined along the dotted line as marked on Pattern A. However, before you stitch B and C together, trim each section to leave ½ in (1 cm) outside the marked edges. Then remove the paper pattern pieces carefully. The short stitches perforate the paper so that it should tear away easily, but you may need to use tweezers to extract small pieces inside points, etc.

7 Join the two halves along the dotted lines as marked on Pattern A. Start at the seams in the center of the kite and work out to each edge in turn. Add borders if you wish to square up the block.

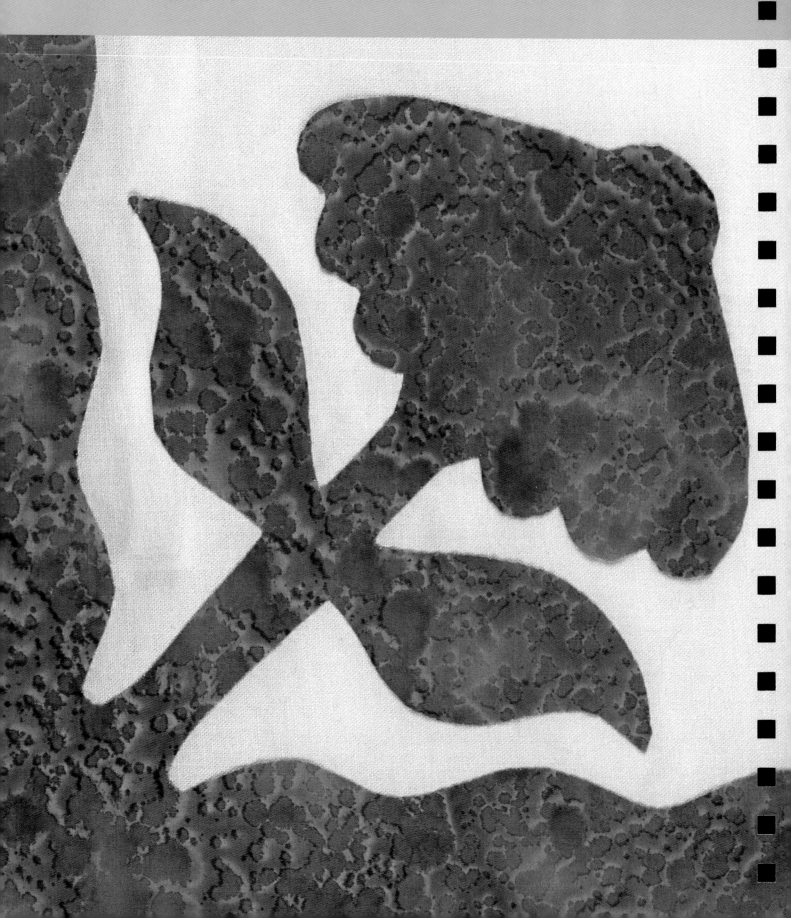

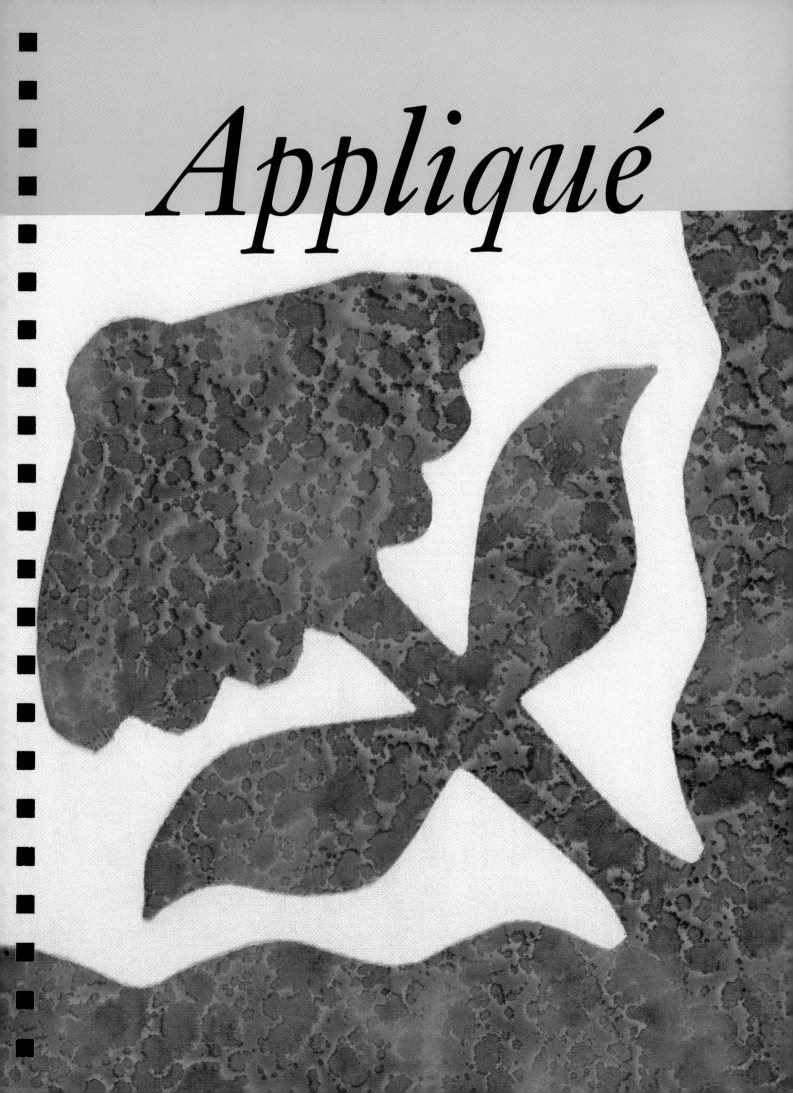

# CHAPTER 4

Appliqué

# Turned-edge appliqué: Dragonfly block

THE TRADITIONAL TECHNIQUE OF TURNING under a narrow seam allowance and slipstitching the edge of a piece of fabric to a background is called turned-edge appliqué. It has been used by stitchers for hundreds of years, and relies on careful stitching to be most effective. A number of methods of have been devised, from using the tip of the needle to turn the edge under to basting with thread or with glue.

1 Cut a 10 in (25 cm) square of background fabric and transfer the dragonfly design to the center of the square.

Trace each element of the design on heatproof Mylar template plastic. Add an overlap where necessary and label each piece. Cut out each piece.

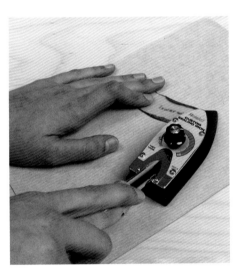

2 Cut a piece of the relevant fabric larger all around than the plastic template. Cut so that the finished piece of fabric will be on the bias. Cut around the template roughly, then trim the piece to allow a generous ⅛ in (3 mm) all around.

3 Place the fabric wrong side up on a piece of cardboard or heavy paper and place the template wrong side up on top of it. With a stiff-bristle brush, paint the edge of the fabric around the template with a strong mixture of powdered starch and water.

4 Starting in the middle of a long edge if possible, use the tip of a small ironing tool to turn the seam allowance of all the edges to be stitched to the wrong side. When all the edges that will be stitched have been turned, press the entire piece on the right side.

**tip** : FRENCH KNOTS
French knots are a valuable embellishment and are especially useful for making eyes.

**1** *Come up at A and wrap the thread around the needle counterclockwise.*

**2** *Make a second wrap in the same direction.*

5 To prepare pieces that are rounded, particularly if they are small, run a single gathering thread around the edge inside the seam allowance and pull it up around the plastic template. Then use the method shown in Step 2 to iron the edges in place securely.

We used this gathering method on the head, thorax, and the point of the tail.

Prepare all the pieces at once and pin them to a spare piece of fabric. This makes the project more portable, and means that you only have to prepare the starch mixture once.

6 With the edges turned and the templates removed, apply the pieces in order, starting with one pair of wings. You may find it easier to work if you use very short pins designed especially for appliqué to hold each piece in place as you work.

Repeat to add the second pair of wings.

7 Apply the tail piece, making sure that you cover the area where the bottom pair of wings meet.

The body piece is applied in the same way and covers the edges of the top pair of wings.

8 Apply the head, covering the top of the body piece so that all the edges are now turned under.

9 Work closely spaced french knots (see Tip, left) in the bulges on each side of the head to make the eyes, and use stem stitch (see page 143) to embroider the antennae.

note: The method shown on pages 106–109 comes from Christine N. Brown, a well-known American teacher and quilt judge, who uses heatproof template plastic to make the pattern pieces. The fabric shapes are then pressed with the templates inside to help them hold their shape and "glued" with starch.

# Broderie perse: Flower block

BRODERIE PERSE, OR PERSIAN EMBROIDERY, is a technique developed in the eighteenth and nineteenth centuries to stretch the precious and expensive chintz fabrics that were being imported into Europe from the East. Motifs were cut from the chintz and applied to a plain, less expensive background fabric to create new designs and combinations of patterns.

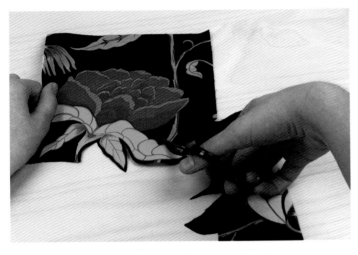

1 Choose a fabric motif and cut it out carefully, leaving a ¼ in (5 mm) seam allowance all around. Then cut a 10 in (25 cm) square of background fabric. Both fabrics should be approximately the same weight, lightweight enough to turn the edges of the motif without difficulty.

2 Pin and then baste the motif in the center of the background square.

note: Broderie perse can also be worked using heavier-weight furnishing or upholstery fabric. It can be zigzagged in place by machine, or buttonhole- or blanket-stitched by hand (see page 117). Motifs can also be positioned using fusible webbing and machine-stitched in place.

3 Using thread that matches the color of the motif, turn under the seam allowance of the motif and apply the motif to the background using slipstitch or blindstitch.

Tips for working turned-edge appliqué appear on pages 106–109.

# Hawaiian appliqué

HAWAIIAN APPLIQUÉ DERIVES FROM papercut patterns that were probably taught to the islanders of Hawaii by German missionaries in the late nineteenth century. Traditional patterns were unique to the individual quiltmaker and are highly stylized and intricate interpretations of natural forms. Using freezer paper (see page 99) to make the pattern speeds up the design process.

*project*: APPLIQUÉ

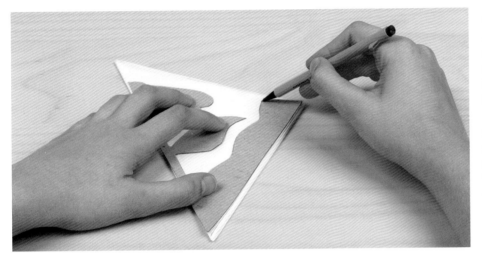

1 Trace the template for the design on page 160 and transfer it to lightweight cardboard or template plastic. It represents one-eighth of the full design. Cut a 13½ in (34 cm) square of freezer paper and fold it into eighths.

Draw around the template to mark one section on the folded freezer paper, making sure the center fold line of the template is on the final fold of the paper. Then staple all eight layers together inside the design lines.

note: To center the fabric squares, fold them in half again. Press lightly, then open and match the fold lines.

2 Cut out the freezer paper pattern and carefully remove all the staples.

3 Cut a 14½ in (37 cm) square of design fabric and one of plain fabric, to create the background when the design is worked. Center the freezer paper pattern on the design fabric square and iron it in place.

Center the square of design fabric wrong side down on the right side of the plain backing fabric and use ½ in (1 cm) basting stitches to baste along the inside of the freezer paper pattern, ¼ in (5 mm) from the edge, through both layers of fabric.

4 Begin to cut away the fabric along the edge of the paper pattern, leaving ⅛ in (3 mm) of design fabric outside the paper. Do NOT trim more than a few inches at a time. Start working along a relatively straight or gently curved section. We have used silk thread to match the top fabric and a milliner's needle.

Turn the ⅛ in (3 mm) allowance under the paper pattern and use tiny slipstitches to apply the design to the background. When you reach an inside curve, clip the allowance to make it lie smooth.

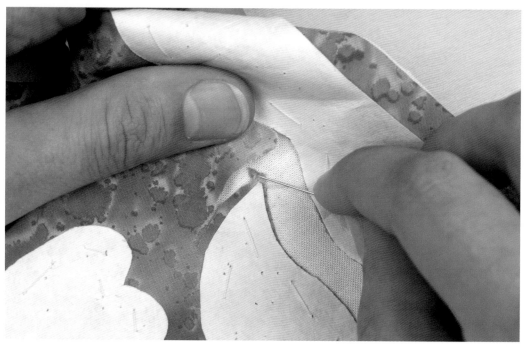

5 Do NOT clip outside curves and points, but fold the fabric under neatly with the point of the needle.

## alternative technique:

If you find it difficult to work with the paper pattern in place, you can make a pattern from plain paper and draw around it onto the design fabric. Then baste the design to the background and cut away a few inches at a time as in Step 4 above as you needle-turn the work.

6 When the appliqué is complete, trim the edges of the square and use your favorite method to make an attractive throw pillow. We have worked a double line of echo quilting around the flowers and quilted the petals separately.

# Raw edge appliqué

NORMALLY THE EDGES OF FABRIC being applied to a background need to be turned under to prevent raveling, but using felt or some tightly woven fabrics, particularly wool, can be effective if the edges are left raw. Bear in mind that both felt and wool, especially in raw-edge work, will not launder well, so they should be used in appropriate situations. The owl pattern is on page 161.

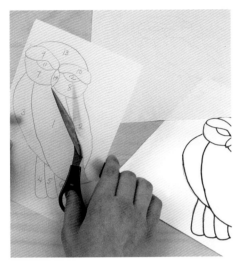

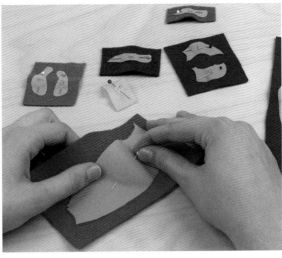

1 Cut a 10 in (25 cm) square of background fabric and transfer the design to the center. Make another copy of the pattern on heavy tracing paper. Number each piece to identify it and to ensure you cut out the fabric on the right side. Cut out each pattern piece separately. You will not need to add seam allowances.

2 Pin the pattern pieces to the relevant fabrics. We have used brightly colored felt. See the Note (right) about using other fabrics.

note: You can use ordinary fabric for raw-edge appliqué, but any woven fabric will fray to a certain extent. If you wish to achieve a frayed look, you can simply apply the fabric in a similar way to the method shown here. If you want to stabilize the edges of the fabric without turning them under, you can use lightweight fusible webbing on the wrong side of each piece and stitch through it. Bear in mind that stitching through the extra layer formed by the webbing is slightly more difficult that stitching only through fabric.

tip: Blanket stitch and its cousin buttonhole stitch provide a way to hold appliqué pieces in place on the background. If you use fabric that frays, you must turn under the raw edge before you stitch.

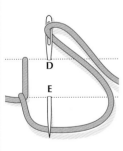

**1** Come up at A, go down at B and come up at C, keeping the thread under the point of the needle from left to right. Pull the thread through.

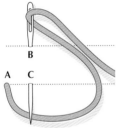

**2** Go down at D to the right of B and come up at E to the right of C, leaving equal spaces between the points. Keep the thread under the point of the needle.

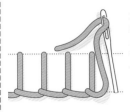

**3** Continue along the row of stitching. Keep the stitches even and equally spaced.

3 Cut out and apply each piece to the background square in turn using thread to match the color of the fabric piece being worked. We have used two strands of cotton embroidery floss. Secure the body and head pieces using blanket stitch (see tip), and use rows of backstitch (see page 57) to apply the wings and tail pieces.

# Reverse appliqué

IN REVERSE APPLIQUÉ THE TOP LAYER of fabric is cut away and secured to the next layer in a technique that is the "reverse" of traditional appliqué, in which a piece of fabric is applied to a background. It is the method used by tribes on opposite sides of the world—the San Blas of Panama and the Hmong of Southeast Asia—to make beautiful and distinctive fabric goods.

2 Trace the pattern for the eagle (see page 162) on the paper side of freezer paper and cut it out. Iron it in the center of the basted fabric squares.

1 Cut the chosen number of fabric squares measuring 10 in (25 cm). Layer them in order—ours are blue, pink, and yellow. Baste them together around the outside edge.

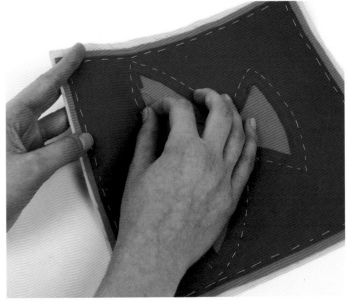

3 Draw around the freezer paper template with a removeable marker and baste around the shape ¼ in (5 mm) from the outside edge. Cut away the shape ¼ in (5 mm) INSIDE the line.

4 Using thread to match the top fabric, turn under the edge of the eagle shape along the marked line and slipstitch it in place.

5 Mark the the cut-out areas on the freezer-paper pattern used in Sep 2. Cut them out and trace the lines for the cut-out areas inside the eagle shape.

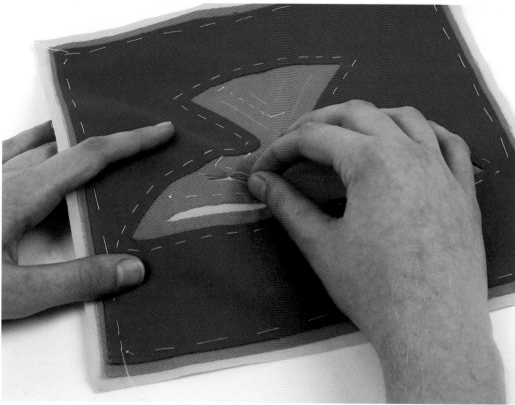

6 Baste between the lines to secure the fabric while you turn under and slipstitch these areas to reveal the third (yellow) fabric. Use thread to match the layer you are stitching, here pink.

**note:** When clipping the seam allowance to work reverse appliqué, cut only halfway down on concave curves. You probably don't need to clip convex curves at all, but inside points should be cut all the way to the stitching line.

7 The orange circle and green triangle are both worked by inserting a small square of fabric into the cut-out area. Use a toothpick to work the small piece into the cut, then turn under and slipstitch the pink layer as before, again using pink thread.

8 The turquoise eye fabric has been cut out using a hole punch and can be anchored in place using an Algerian eye stitch or a circular buttonhole stitch.

# Inlay appliqué

INLAY OR CHANNEL APPLIQUÉ is a relatively new variation of reverse appliqué (pages 118–121). Simple designs work well, but complex patterns of lines can also be stitched to create channels of contrasting color ¼ in (5 mm) wide in the top fabric. The method shown here uses two layers of fabric—cut away the back fabric if you wish to make a thinner block.

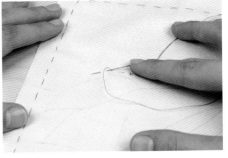

**tip:** You need to draw only one line when transferring the pattern to fabric—this line will be cut and the seam allowances turned back on each side to create the channel. Use small sharp scissors to cut the lines.

1 Cut a 10 in (25 cm) square of background fabric. Trace the swan pattern (page 163) and transfer it to the back-ground square. Because you will be cutting along the marked lines, you can use any type of marker you prefer.

Cut a 9 in (23 cm) square of contrasting fabric and baste it around the edges with the right side of the contrasting square to the wrong side of the background fabric.

2 Baste along both sides of the marked design ¼ in (5 mm) from the lines. Use a contrasting thread for clarity and keep the knots on the top of the work.

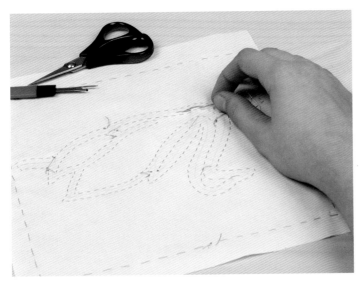

3 When the outline basting has been completed, use a seam ripper to cut along the design line. Work carefully, cutting only a short section at a time to prevent fraying. Use the tip of a needle to turn under one raw edge and slipstitch it in place (see page 57) with a thread that matches the background fabric. Work all along one edge, then work the other edge.

4 When the edges have all been stitched under, remove the basting. Press the square gently from the wrong side. If you wish, you can trim away the contrasting fabric from outside the stitched lines to reduce the bulk.

# Shadow appliqué

SHADOW APPLIQUÉ IS SOMETIMES called shadow quilting. Very thin silk organza or voile is laid over the design and stitched in place to create muted effects, and embellishments can be added. The fabrics in the underlayer need to be bright and clear, or the colors will be knocked back and may virtually disappear when the overlay is added.

1 Cut a 10 in (25 cm) square of background fabric. Trace the butterfly design (see page 164) and transfer it to the center of the background square with a fine-line marker. Trace each section of the design separately on freezer paper and cut them out.

2 Iron the shiny side of the freezer paper shapes to the right side of the appropriate fabrics and cut each one out. Cut slightly inside the marked line—the pieces should be separated by a tiny area of background.

3 Fit each one onto the appropriate background area and secure it in position with a thin layer of fabric glue.

4 When all the colored shapes are in place, cut a 10 in (25 cm) square of organza to use as the overlay. Baste the organza square over the background so the colored shapes show through.

5 Stitch between each section of the design and outline the entire shape using a fine thread, preferably silk sewing thread, and a small running stitch (see page 57). Embroider the butterfly's antennae using the same stitch and thread.

note: Silk organza is the most appropriate type of fabric to use for the overlay. Cotton and polyester versions tend to be too thick.

# Machine appliqué

THERE ARE A NUMBER OF METHODS for working machine appliqué (see the alternative method, opposite). Here we have used fusible webbing to secure the shapes to the background fabric and finished the edges with a machine satin stitch. We have used machine embroidery thread and changed it to match the color of the piece it is outlining.

1 Cut a 10 in (25 cm) square of background fabric. Trace the beetle design (see page 165) and transfer it to the center of the background square.

In order to transfer the fabrics to the background, you must reverse the tracing. One way to do this is to photocopy the drawing, turn it over, and draw around the outlines on the reverse side.

2 Trace each element of the design, separately and back to front, on the paper side of a piece of fusible webbing. If the same fabric is used for several pieces, gang them together in a group, leaving space to cut them out separately. There is no need to add seam allowances. We have cut the large dark purple piece as one and created the beetle's "wings" by stitching down the center.

Cut out each section with a margin of webbing around it, and follow the manufacturer's instructions to iron each piece to the wrong side of the fabric.

3 Cut out the fabric pieces one by one and fuse them in position on the background square. The pieces in machine appliqué work usually butt up against one another, but if there are any overlaps, make sure you fuse the underneath layer first.

4 When all the pieces are fused in place, set your sewing machine to work a very narrow satin stitch to outline all the edges. Using an open foot designed for appliqué or embroidery makes it easier to see the work as you stitch.

# Bias strip appliqué

APPLIQUÉ IN WHICH BIAS STRIPS are used to outline shapes is found in several different types of applied work, mainly Celtic patterns with their under-and-over spiral designs and stained glass work, in which the bias strips mock the leading in church windows. You can use the iron-on commercial tape shown here, or make your own strips to a variety of widths.

1 Cut a 10 in (25 cm) square of background fabric. Trace the goose design (see page 166) and transfer it to the center of the background square.

Trace the head and body pieces on the paper side of fusible webbing, cut them out, and iron them to the wrong side of the chosen fabric.

2 Cut out the fabric shapes—there is no need for seam allowances—and follow the manufacturer's directions to iron them onto the background square.

3 We have used a commercial iron-on bias strip (see Note below) to outline the goose and to create the legs and tail feathers. Plan the order in which you apply the strips—wherever possible, try to cover raw ends with another strip.

Start with the legs and tail feathers, ironing them carefully in turn.

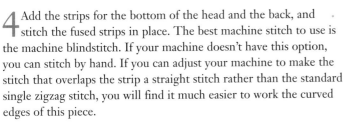

**note:** Available in quilt stores and good notions departments in a limited selection of colors, Quick Bias consists of a ¼ in (5 mm) strip of bias fabric backed with a strip of fusible webbing that can be curved into a variety of shapes. It is widely used for stained glass and Celtic appliqué designs.

4 Add the strips for the bottom of the head and the back, and stitch the fused strips in place. The best machine stitch to use is the machine blindstitch. If your machine doesn't have this option, you can stitch by hand. If you can adjust your machine to make the stitch that overlaps the strip a straight stitch rather than the standard single zigzag stitch, you will find it much easier to work the curved edges of this piece.

5 Apply the head, neck, and belly outline as one continuous strip. Iron it in place carefully and stitch as before. It will cover the ends of all the other strips.

# CHAPTER 5

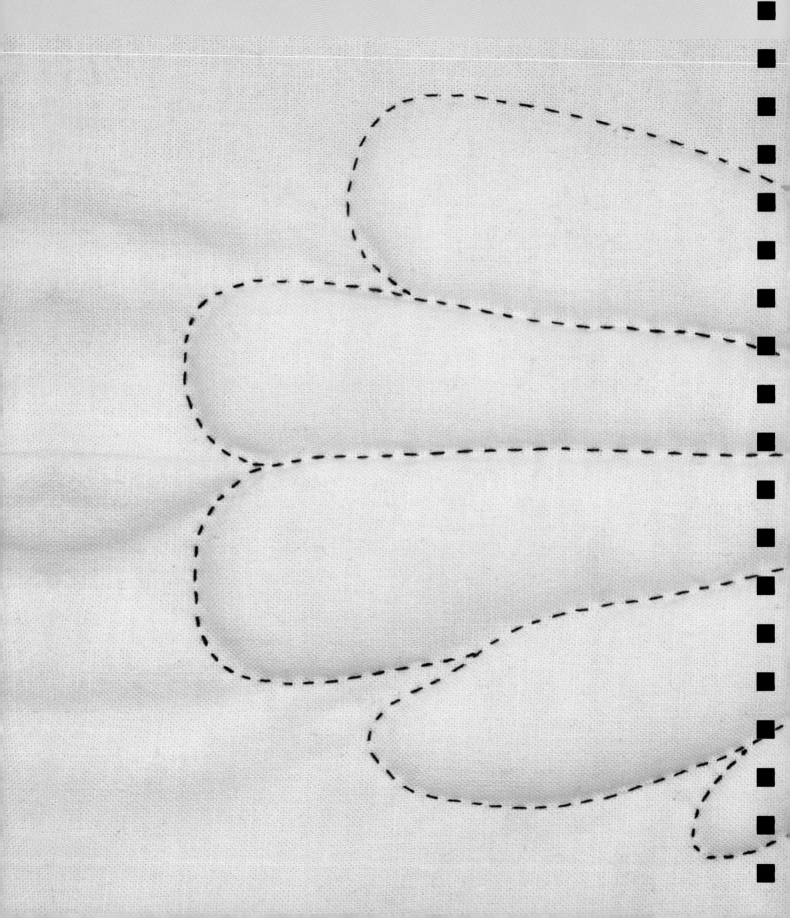

# Quilting

# Hand quilting steps

BEAUTIFUL HAND QUILTING IS CONSIDERED the pinnacle of the quiltmaker's art. The best-known method of hand quilting, known as "rocking," takes much practice to perfect, but the results can make it worth the effort. Most quilters work using a frame, but others prefer frameless quilting. In either method, you will need protection for your stitching finger, and you may want to cover your stitching thumb and various digits on your non-stitching hand, which will be underneath the work, as well.

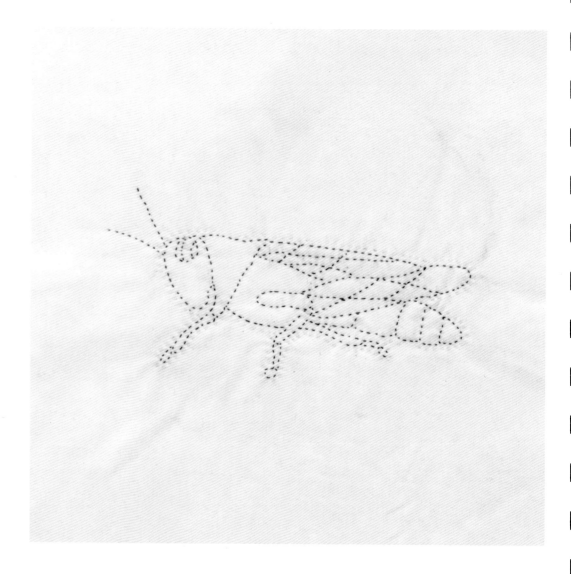

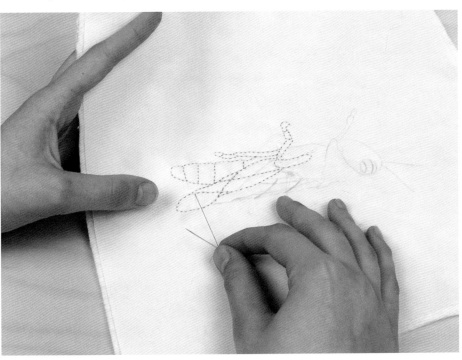

1 Cut a 10 in (25 cm) square of background fabric. Trace the cricket pattern (see page 167) and transfer it onto the right side of the fabric using a washable marker. Cut a 10 in (25 cm) square of batting.

2 Baste the fabric and batting together. Work out from the center diagonally, then vertically and horizontally.

3 Using small quilting stitches, quilt all the marked lines with quilting thread. We have used a contrasting color for the outline quilting. When the outlining has been completed, remove the marking lines. We have outline-quilted the outside edge of the design in quilting thread the same color as the background fabric.

**tip:** HAND QUILTING
Hand quilting looks similar to a small running stitch, but it is not the same. Every quilter has a slightly different way of making the stitches, called "rocking," and practice is necessary.

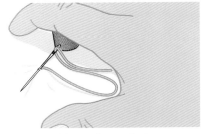

*Insert the tip of the needle straight down through all the layers and tilt it back up as straight as possible, again piercing all the layers.*

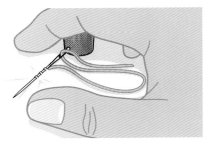

*Repeat the rocking motion to take three or four stitches onto the needle, then pull it through the fabric before repeating the process.*

# Tied quilting: Log Cabin

TYING IS A QUICK METHOD OF HOLDING the layers of a quilt together. It is found on many historical quilts, especially those in everyday use around the home. Log cabin quilts with their many seams were often tied. Here we show the technique for making a simple Log Cabin block and tying it to make a holiday-themed table mat.

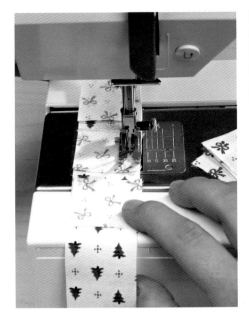  

1 To make the Log Cabin design, cut four 1½ in (4 cm) center squares. Ours are light. Cut a strip of the first light fabric (Fabric 1) 1½ in (4 cm) wide.

Chain piece (see page 42) by laying the squares one after the other on the strip and stitch. Cut apart and press each unit.

2 Place each unit on the remaining strip of Fabric 1 and stitch as in Step 2 to add the second side of the block. Cut the units apart and press.

3 The third strip is a dark fabric (Fabric 2). Cut a 1½ in (4 cm) strip and chain piece as before.

note: Tying is probably the best-known type of "utility" quilting, in which the object was to secure the quilt layers together effectively in the shortest time possible. Big-stitch quilting is another popular utility technique, which is often found on quilts made by African-American quiltmakers. It is also a quick method, one that creates fascinating textures on the surface of a quilt.

4 Finish the first "round" of logs in the same way by chain-piecing the necessary number of blocks.

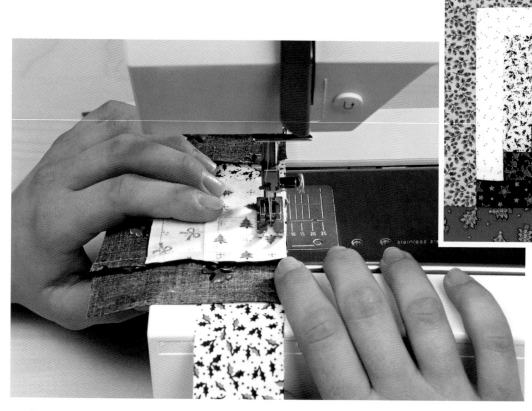

**5** Cut and add the second light strip in the same way. Then continue to complete four rounds of strips, finishing with the two middle-value fabrics. The cream fabric will create a cross in the center of the finished piece, while the red makes an attractive inner border (inset).

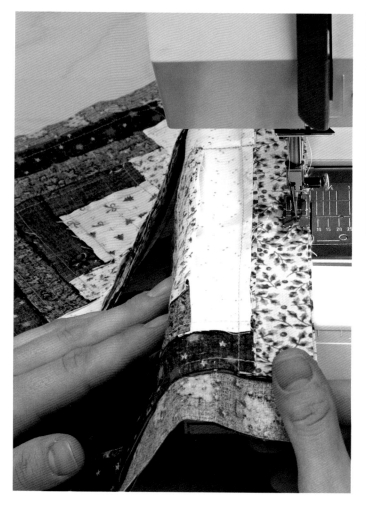

**tip:** A number of threads can be used to tie a quilt. We have worked with several strands of cotton embroidery floss, but fine string or twine, pearl cotton embroidery thread, or some yarns can all be used. Bear in mind, though, that some yarns made from synthetic fibers are prone to coming untied.

**6** Combine the four finished blocks by stitching them together two by two and then joining them into one.

7 Cut a 2 in (5 cm) strip for the border and add it following the intructions on pages 58–59. Cut squares of backing fabric and batting the same size as the finished Log Cabin—ours is 21 in (53 cm)—and bag out the piece following the instructions on page 65.

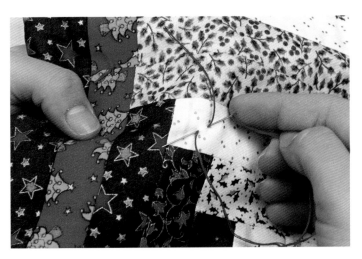

8 To tie the quilt, cut a long piece of your chosen thread. We have used red stranded embroidery floss, but you can choose quilting thread, yarn, or even string if appropriate. Thread an embroidery needle and working from the top, take the thread through all layers to the back, leaving a tail of thread on top. Bring it back to the front near the place where you started and repeat to make a double stitch.

9 Tie the thread with a double knot. Cut the thread and move the needle to the next point of entry, repeating the stitching and tying at evenly spaced intervals.

# Sashiko

SASHIKO IS A TRADITIONAL JAPANESE quilting technique that is frequently classified as a utility method (see Note, page 135), but its intricate regular patterns lift it out of the ordinary. Originally used to secure layers of fabric used in workclothes worn by farmers, fishermen, and firemen, its practitioners developed highly stylized designs that create wonderful decorative patterns.

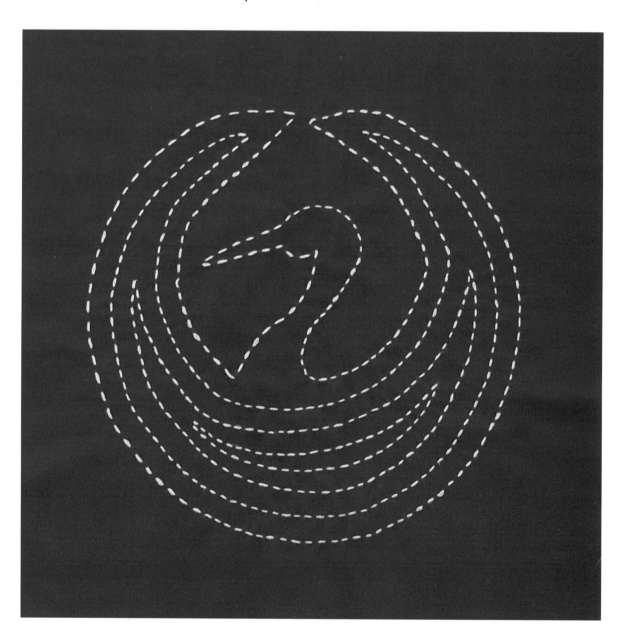

note: While sashiko is traditionally worked in white thread on dark blue indigo cloth, it can be highly effective when stitched with dark thread on light fabric, such as blue, red, or dark green on white or cream. Most of the traditional designs are based on plant or animal forms.

1 Cut a 10 in (25 cm) square of background fabric—dark blue is traditional—and one of a lightweight backing fabric. Baste them together around all four sides.

Trace the crane design (see page 168) on the paper side of freezer paper. Cut it out and iron it to the background square. Draw around the edge with a removeable marker and remove the freezer-paper template.

2 Begin stitching along the marked outline. The special thread designed for sashiko is the best choice for this type of work, but a fine pearl cotton can be used.

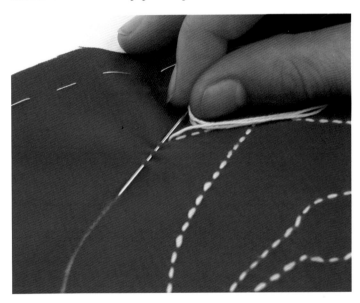

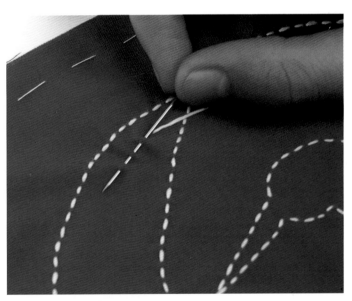

3 Work all around the outline. The ideal is to make the stitches, and the spaces between them, even.

4 When the outlining has been completed, decide where you wish to place the interior stitching. Sashiko can be worked in a geometric way, but in the rounded shape of the crane, we have chosen to echo the shape of the wings. Fill in with as many rows as you feel look good.

# Trapunto

TRAPUNTO IS ALSO KNOWN AS stuffed quilting. It is widely used to pad areas of a quilt, creating relief designs that are wonderfully sculptural and three-dimensional. The areas of padding can be thickly or thinly stuffed depending on the desired effect. Padded sections are completed before the full quilt is batted, backed, and quilted.

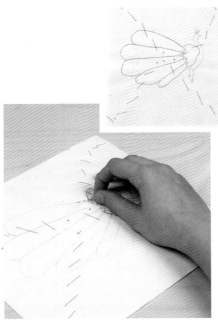

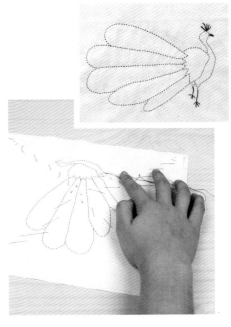

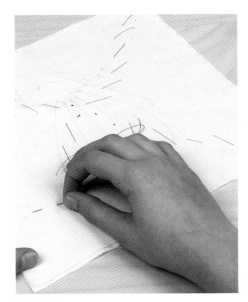

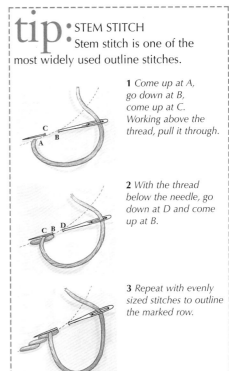

1 Cut 10 in (25 cm) squares of background fabric and lightweight backing fabric. Trace the peacock design (see page 169) and transfer it to the center of the background square using a washable marker. Baste the background and backing squares together.

2 Begin outline quilting around the wing area. (Inset) Outline-quilt the tail feathers.

3 Outline-quilt the body, and stem stitch (see page 143) the beak, crown, eye, and legs.

(Inset) Remove the basting and the marking lines following the manufacturer's instructions.

4 Turn the work to the back and make a small slit in the wing area through the backing fabric only. Stuff the wing area with small pieces of batting or other stuffing, using a toothpick or bodkin carefully to work the stuffing into the pointed areas.

5 Stuff each segment in the same way in turn, paying careful attention to the bird's head, neck, and body. When all the outline-quilted areas have been filled, stitch up the slits with herringbone or crossed stitches. Use a thread to match the backing ... we have stitched in a contrasting color for clarity. The block is now complete and ready to be incorporated into a quilt.

## tip: STEM STITCH
Stem stitch is one of the most widely used outline stitches.

**1** Come up at A, go down at B, come up at C. Working above the thread, pull it through.

**2** With the thread below the needle, go down at D and come up at B.

**3** Repeat with evenly sized stitches to outline the marked row.

# Corded quilting

CORDED QUILTING IS A VARIATION of trapunto (see pages 142–143) in which channels are stitched through the top fabric and a thin backing layer and some type of cording is pulled through the channel, working on the back of the piece, to create a delicate raised line. The cording can range from string to yarn to a special type of quilting wool, which is an untwisted yarn especially designed to give a firm but soft effect. Working in a contrasting thread gives a different look from a piece stitched with matching thread.

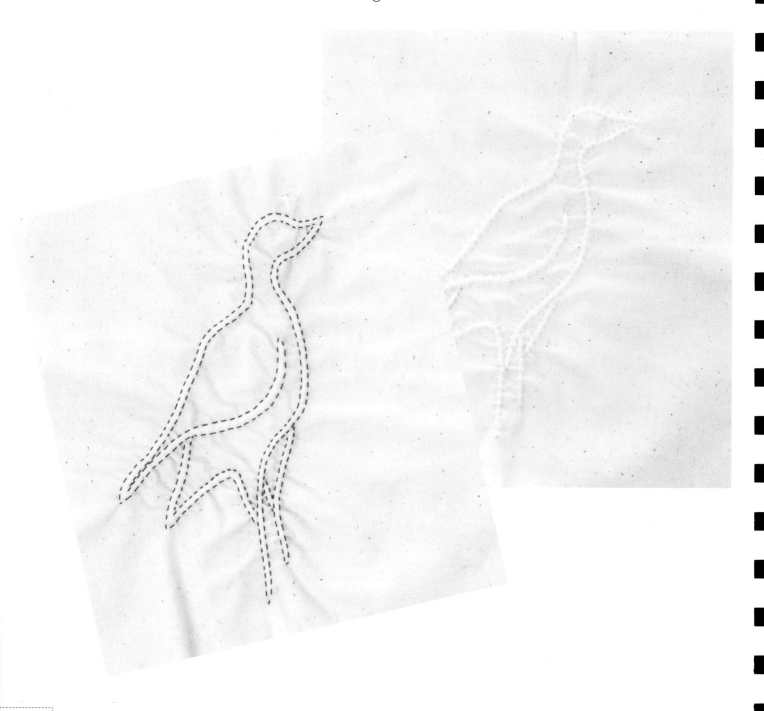

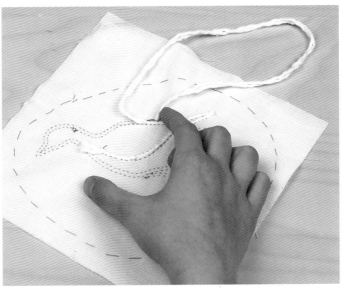

1 Cut a 10 in (25 cm) background square. Cut a 9 in (23 cm) backing square of loosely woven cloth (cheesecloth/butter muslin).

Trace the stork design (see page 170) and transfer it to the background square using a removeable marker. Center the backing square on the wrong side of the background square and baste them together.

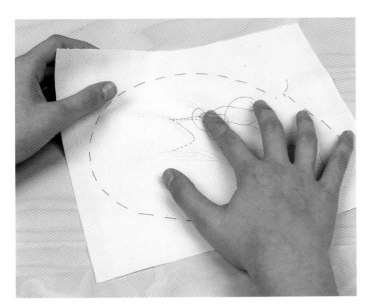

2 Using a small running stitch (see page 57), outline the design to make a channel, paying careful attention to places where the lines meet. When you have completed stitching the outline, remove the marking lines following the manufacturer's instructions.

3 Thread a tapestry needle with the chosen yarn or cord. Working from the back, slide yarn through the channel, leaving a short tail at each end. The needle will slip through the holes in the backing fabric easily, but it may be necessary to bring it out and reinsert it occasionally, especially on the outward curves, even gentle ones. When the cording is completed, remove the basting threads.

# Machine quilting

MACHINE QUILTING CAN BE used to stitch grids of straight-line quilting, to make meandering background patterns, or to create pictorial designs or patterns. All require practice, and when you are stitching a large piece of work, you will need plenty of table space set at the correct height.

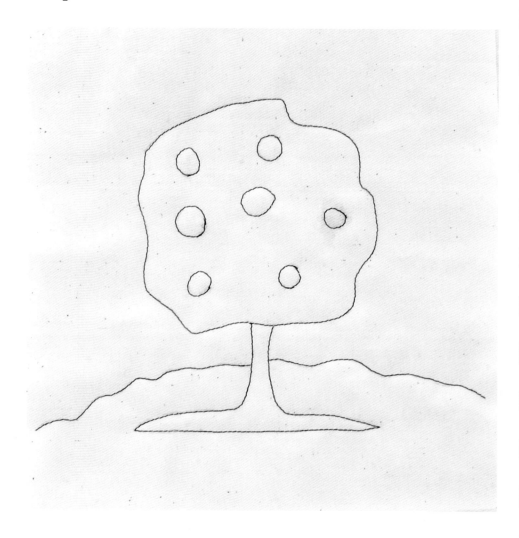

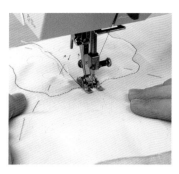

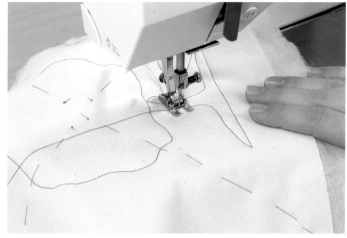

1 Cut a 10 in (25 cm) square of background fabric and a slightly larger batting square. Use a washable marker to transfer the design (see page 171) to the center of the fabric square. Baste the fabric and batting together.

Choose a suitable quilting, appliqué, or embroidery foot and put it on your machine. Place the square in the machine and choose a starting point. We have used the top left-hand corner of the trunk where it meets the tree. Turn the wheel by hand to take one stitch and stop. Pull the end of the bobbin thread up to the top of the work and hold both threads gently as you begin to stitch. You can take both thread up to the top of the work and hold both threads gently as you begin to stitch. You can take both threads through to the back of the work to tie them off when you have finished the quilting, or you can take several stitches with the stitch length set at 0 to start and finish.

2 To quilt the tree and its trunk, stitch carefully around the marked outline. Our machine is set on a medium-length stitch. Work the tree first, then with the needle down, turn the square and stitch the trunk.

3 Stitch the background hill the same way, starting at the tree trunk on each side.

tip: The choice of thread and needle is crucial to the look of your work. The needle should be as fine as possible for the thread to go through the eye easily, and should be replaced often before it becomes dull and tears the fabric.

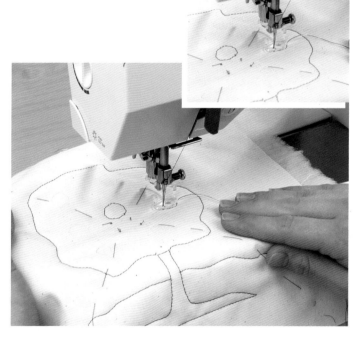

4 To work the fruit on the tree, use free-motion quilting. Drop the feed dogs on the machine and position the center fruit under the needle. Set the stitch length on 0. Take a stitch as in Step 2 and pull the thread to the top. Then using free-motion, work around each fruit in turn (inset). It is not always necessary to turn the work; stitch by moving the fabric. Always practice on a scrap of fabric and batting before starting on the actual piece. This will give you a feel for how the machine is responding and allow you to establish a rhythm. Getting a balance between the speed of the machine, which should be fairly fast, and the speed of your movements, which are slower and deliberate, and which must be smooth, is the key to machine quilting.

Remove the basting and the marking, and trim the batting to the same size as the fabric square.

# Quilt-as-you-go

WORKING PATCHWORK DIRECTLY ONTO LAYERS of batting and backing creates a piece that needs no further quilting. The method works particularly well on patchwork assembled from strips, such as the medallion, or frame, hanging here, and is ideal when making Log Cabin blocks (see pages 134–137). The overall effect will resemble quilting in the ditch.

1 Cut out the center panel, leaving a ¼ in (5mm) seam allowance all around. You can also use a patchwork or appliqué block for the center.

Cut a background square of batting and backing the size of the finished piece plus seam allowances—ours is 20 in (50 cm) square. Baste them together around all four sides.

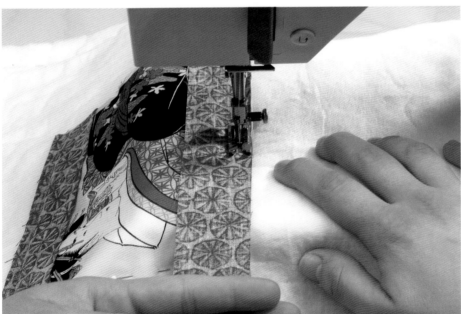

2 Cut the first strip—ours is red and 1½ in (4 cm) wide. Center the medallion on the batting and apply the first strip all around. Stitch the sides first, fingerpress them open, and then apply the top and bottom strips. By stitching through all the layers, you are quilting as you work.

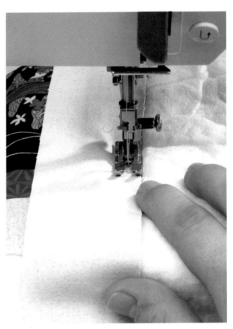

3 Add the second border—ours is yellow and 2 in (5 cm) wide—in the same way, and fingerpress it open.

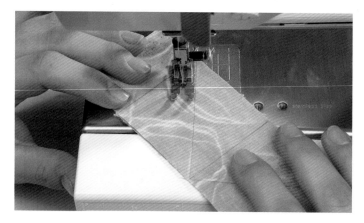

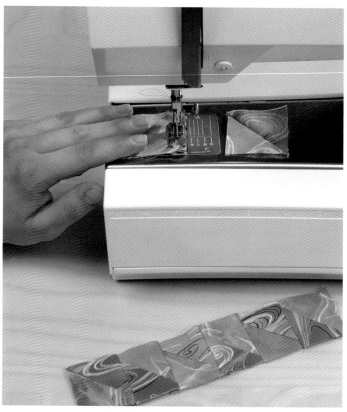

4 To make the pieced border, cut pink and brown strips 2¼ in (6 cm) wide. On the wrong side of the lighter-colored strip, mark seven 2¼ in (6 cm) squares along the length. Mark diagonal lines in one direction only from opposite corners. Make fourteen triangle squares as shown on page 43.

5 Join the triangle squares to make two strips of seven squares each, alternating colors as shown to make two pieced borders.

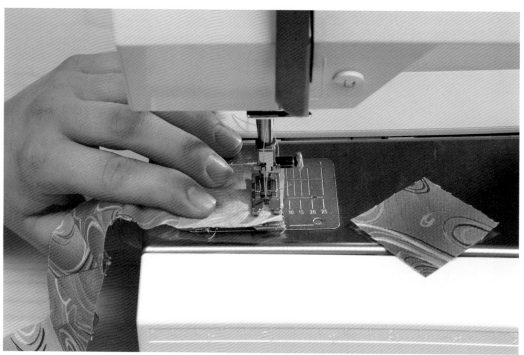

6 The pieced borders are 1¾ in (4.5 cm) wide. Cut two squares from each fabric used to make the triangle squares and add one of each color to opposite ends of the strips as shown, matching pink to pink and brown to brown.

**tip:** Remember that the batting and backing will shrink as you work, so make sure you cut them large enough to compensate. You can trim them to the finished size when the piecing has been completed.

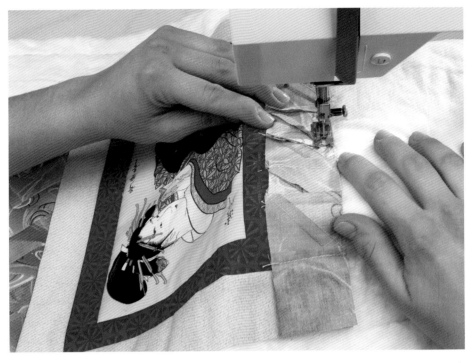

7 Add the pieced borders to the sides of the bordered medallion and press them open.

8 Then cut 2 in (5 cm) strips for the fourth (blue) and fifth (black) borders. Cut four 2 in (5 cm) red squares and four 2 in (5 cm) yellow squares. Following the instructions for adding corner squares on page 59, add the fourth and fifth borders with corner squares on all four sides.

Trim all the thread ends on the back of the work. Sewing through all the layers at once means that the piece is now quilted.

Press the final hanging and cut 1½ in (4 cm) straight strips for the binding. Trim the batting and backing to the finished measurement. Add single binding as shown on page 66.

# Using blocks

BLOCKS ARE GENERALLY MADE to be set together into quilts or wall hangings. They can be incorporated into articles of clothing or made into cushions and other items of home furnishings as well. Here, we have taken some of the blocks made in this chapter and turned them into quilts. Information about assembling quilts can be found on pages 58–67.

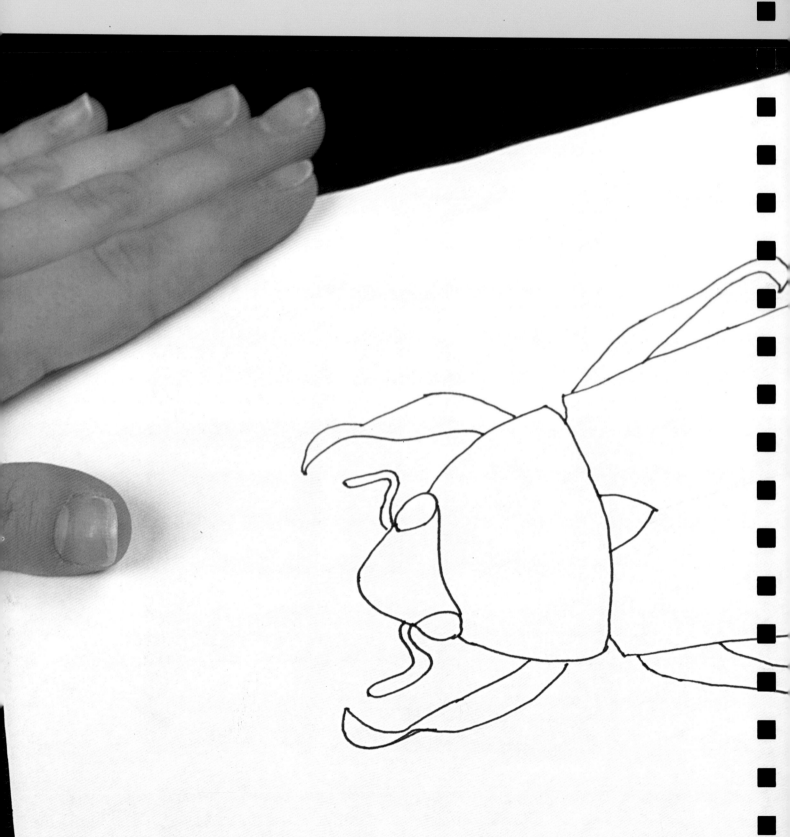

# CHAPTER 6

# Templates

# Using templates

Templates are the patterns from which designs are worked. The first step in using templates is to copy the design either by photocopying or scanning it or tracing it by hand. Be sure to transfer all the marks on the patterns, such as the lines on the templates opposite that indicate the notches used for matching.

Templates may need to be enlarged (or sometimes but rarely reduced). This can easily be done on a photocopier with a reduce/enlarge function.

Paper patterns can be glued to lightweight cardboard to make them sturdier, or you can use template plastic, a translucent heavy film that can be drawn on and which is long-lasting, especially useful if you are making multiple copies of backing papers or fabric pieces, as in the English paper pieced mat on pages 98–99, for example.

Make sure you transfer the pattern to the correct side of the fabric. Usually you will mark around the template on the right side of the material, and you will be instructed otherwise if required. In some cases, you will need to use a removable marker, but if you are marking on the wrong side of the fabric, this is not necessary. Just make sure you use light marks that will not show through the fabric on the right side.

Other types of templates and ways of marking are discussed on pages 36, 37, 49, and 50.

**ENGLISH PAPER PIECING: page 98**

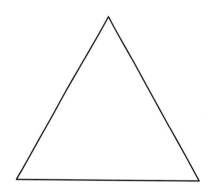

**CURVES: DRUNKARDS' PATH: page 82**

**PICTORIAL LANDSCAPE: page 94**

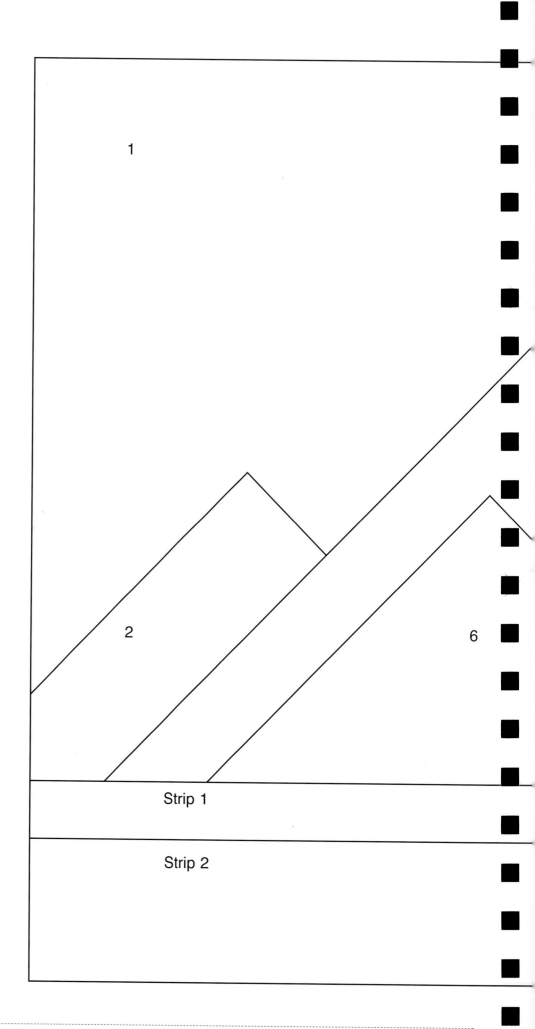

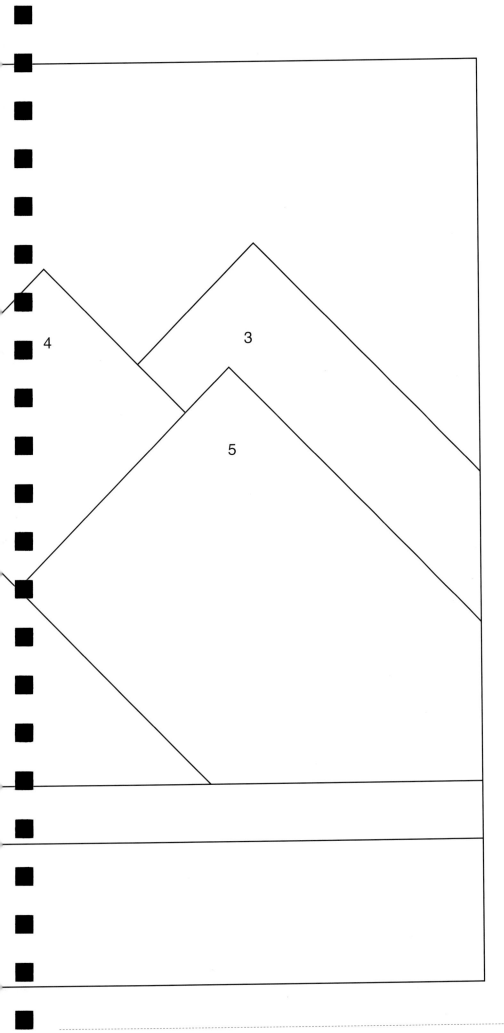

**FOUNDATION PIECING: KITE BLOCK: page 100**

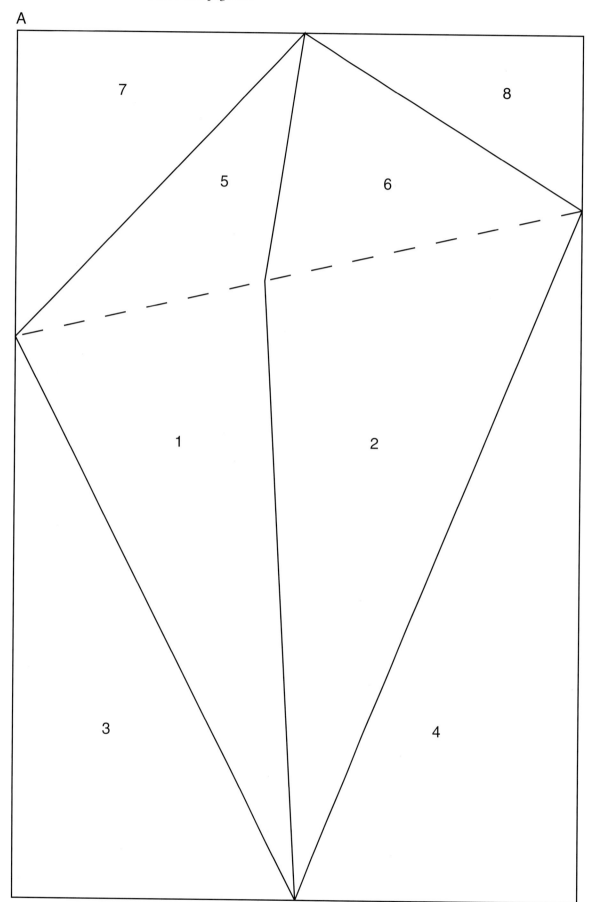

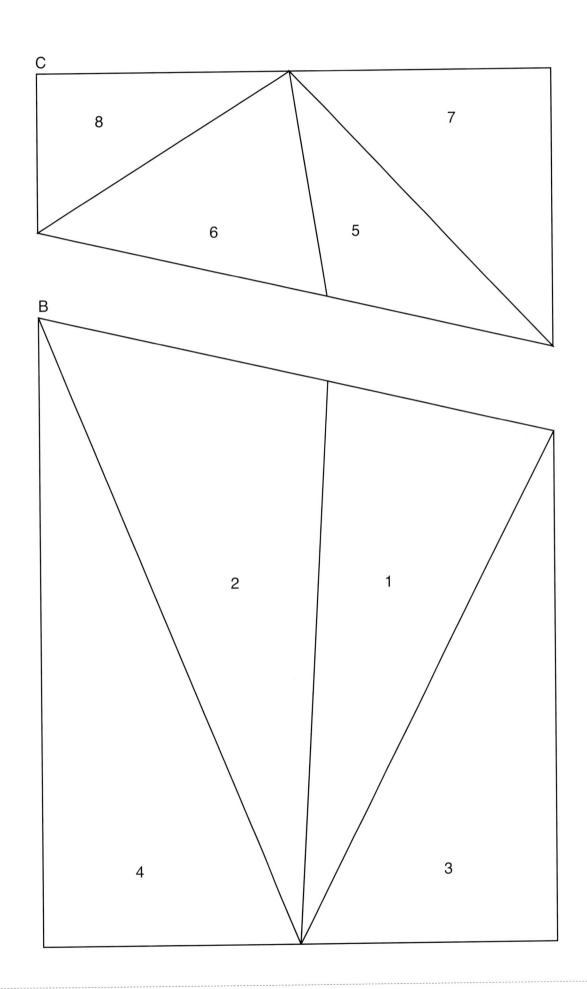

**HAWAIIAN APPLIQUÉ: page 112**

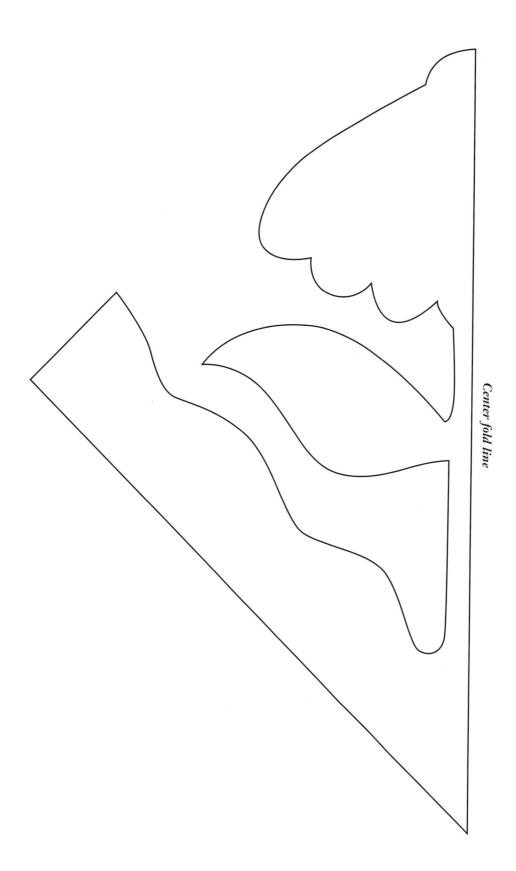

Center fold line

**RAW EDGE APPLIQUÉ: page 116**

**REVERSE APPLIQUÉ: page 118**

**INLAY APPLIQUÉ: page 122**

**SHADOW APPLIQUÉ: page 124**

**MACHINE APPLIQUÉ: page 126**

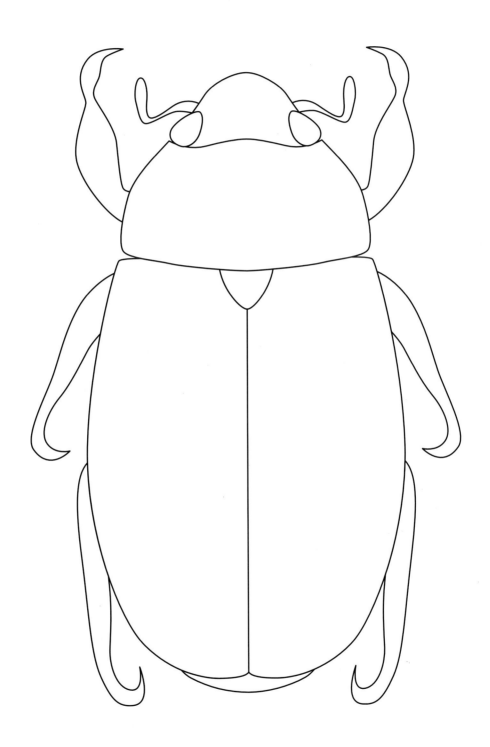

**BIAS STRIP APPLIQUÉ: page 128**

**HAND QUILTING: page 132**

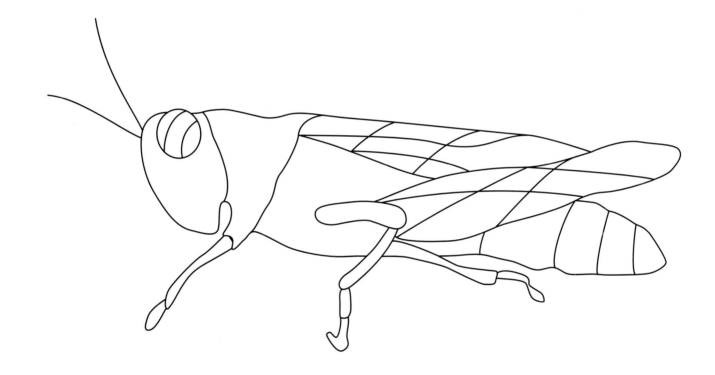

**SASHIKO: page 138**

**TRAPUNTO: page 140**

**CORDED QUILTING: page 142**

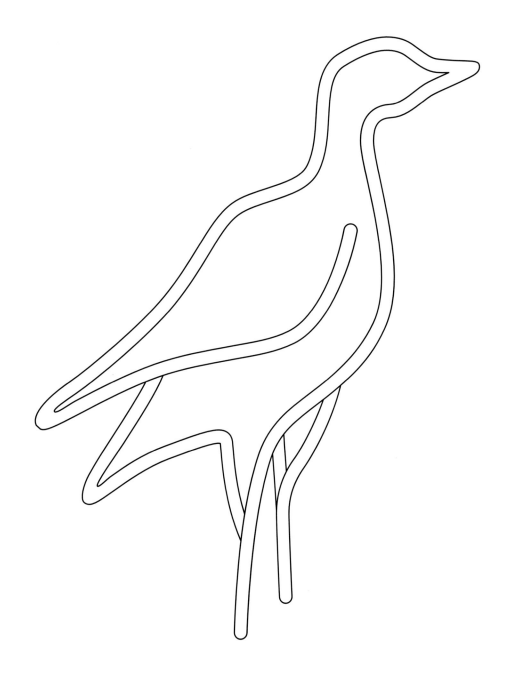

**MACHINE QUILTING: page 144**

# Glossary

**appliqué** Applying fabric shapes or motifs to a background fabric by hand or machine.

**backing** Literally, the back of a quilt, which can either be a single piece of cloth or pieced. It can even be a separate quilt, making it a double-sided quilt.

**bagging** Finishing a quilt by sewing the layers together around the edges before turning it right side out through a small opening. This technique eliminates the need for a separate binding round the edges.

**Baltimore album** Traditional type of highly elaborate and very colorful appliqué quilt made mainly in the area around Baltimore, Maryland, between about 1840 and 1860.

**basting** Technique used to hold the layers of a quilt together while it is being quilted. Traditionally done with large single-thread stitches, now can be accomplished using safety pins; basting spray, a special spray-on adhesive that washes out; or plastic ties shot from a "basting gun."

**batting** The middle layer of a quilt, lying between the top and the backing. Traditionally made of cotton fibers or wool, now processed into a felted material that can be purchased precut or by length from a roll. Made from cotton, polyester, or a combination of the two; also available, usually by special order, are wool and silk.

**bias** The diagonal line between the straight horizontal and vertical grains of a fabric, cut at a 45-degree angle to the straight grain. It stretches very easily, and should be handled with care.

**big-stitch quilting** (see utility quilting)

**binding** The way in which the outside edges of a quilt are finished. It can be a strip of fabric cut either on the straight grain or on the bias. Quilts can also be bound by turning the raw edges to the inside of the quilt, or by taking the edge of the backing to the front, or vice versa, to cover the raw edges.

**block** The basic unit that is combined with other blocks to make up many quilts. Often made from patchwork, blocks can also be plain or appliquéd. The way patterned blocks are joined together determines the overall design of the quilt.

**border** Strips of fabric, plain or pieced, applied to the edges of a quilt. They create a "frame" to hold the design together visually.

**broderie perse** A type of traditional appliqué in which motifs are cut from one fabric and applied to a background fabric, usually plain.

**calico** (US) A type of printed fabric, usually cotton, that is widely used in quiltmaking. (UK) A plain cotton fabric, usually cream (unbleached) or white (bleached), used for backgrounds and backings.

**chain piecing** A fast way to assemble patchwork blocks, accomplished by sewing patches together in a chain without breaking the thread between units. The unbroken threads hold the pieces together until the chain is cut to assemble the next step.

**color wheel** A round device used to visualize the way colors relate to one another.

**complementary colors** Colors that occur opposite each other on the color wheel.

**contrast** The differences in tone and value between fabrics used in a quilt, generally measured as dark, medium, and light, which delineate depth and pattern.

**corded quilting** Traditional type of quilting in which a double channel is stitched on the top and backing layers of fabric. Yarn or cord is then threaded through the channel raising the surface and delicately outlining the motif.

**crazy quilt** A type of patchwork quilt, very popular in Victorian times, in which pieces of odd-shaped fabric are joined to make a jumbled abstract design. Traditionally made by sewing the patches onto a foundation backing, crazy quilts typically were made from silk, cotton, velvet, and wool and embellished with beads, lace, ribbons, and elaborate embroidery.

**edge to edge** A method of joining blocks in a quilt by setting them side by side with no separating strips (sashing).

**foundation piecing** A technique for sewing pieces to a foundation, usually of paper or fabric, either for stability or to facilitate joining small or irregular shapes. Usually worked from the back.

**four-patch** One of the simplest block configurations. Each block consists of four smaller units, usually squares of equal size, and often broken down into even smaller units with color alternating.

**frame quilt** A type of quilt in which strips of plain or pieced fabric are placed in concentric rows around a central block or motif to "frame" the center. The technique can also be used to enlarge an individual block. (see also medallion)

**frame, quilting** A wooden or plastic frame on which a quilt is mounted to stetch and secure the layers for quilting. A frame can be round, D-shaped, oval, square, or rectangular.

**freezer paper** A waxed paper, with a paper side that can be drawn on and a shiny side that can be ironed to fabric temporarily. Widely used in appliqué work, it is sold by the roll in supermarkets to wrap food for the freezer, and it is also available in many quilt stores.

**fusible webbing** An iron-on adhesive with a paper side that can be drawn on. It can be ironed onto fabric shapes that can then be applied to a background fabric.

**grain** Term used to describe the direction of woven threads in a piece of fabric. Straight grain refers to lengthwise or crosswise threads; when fabric is cut on the diagonal, it is called the bias.

**Hawaiian appliqué** Type of appliqué based on symmetrical, usually eight-sided designs. It originated in Hawaii toward the end of the nineteenth century and has much in common with schrenschnitte paper-cut work.

**Italian quilting** (see corded quilting)

**kit quilt** Type of quilt made from a kit. A particular style of floral kit quilts, almost all appliqué, were popular in the 1920s to 1940s.

**meander quilting** A popular type of machine quilting pattern that relies on curving, seemingly random lines of stitching that should ideally not cross each other. Widely used to provide background quilting to large areas, meandering flattens the surface.

**medallion** (see frame quilt)

**miter** A corner that meets at a 45-degree angle.

**monochromatic** A color scheme that relies on only one color but which uses different values and various tints and shades of that color for its effect.

**mosaic** Sometimes referred to as "one-patch" patterns, mosaic is a term that describes work created from small colored pieces, originally tiles, to make a geometric or pictorial design. Such patterns rely heavily on different color values for their effectiveness.

**muslin** **(US)** A plain cotton fabric, usually cream (unbleached) or white (bleached), used for backgrounds and backings. (UK) A fine loosely woven fabric similar to cheesecloth. Also called butter muslin.

**nine-patch** Block with a configuration of three rows of three units. It is one of the most versatile and widely seen types of block.

**paper piecing, English** A traditional technique in which individual fabric shapes are basted to backing paper shapes to stabilize them. It is often used to join hexagons, triangles, and diamonds, all of which have set-in angles and bias raw edges that are very prone to stretching out of shape.

**patchwork** Sewing together (piecing) fabric shapes to create a new piece of cloth.

**piecing** Another term for patchwork.

**primary colors** The three colors—red, yellow, and blue—from which all other colors can be created.

**quilt** A type of textile made from three layers—top, middle, and backing—and sewn together through all the layers. The top and backing can either be plain, pieced, or appliquéd or even a mixture; the middle is usually referred to as batting or wadding.

**quilt-as-you-go** A traditional technique in which blocks are worked with batting and backing in place. Finished blocks are then joined in rows to make the quilt.

**quilting** A specialized type of running stitch used to hold the layers of a quilt together. Western tradition aims to achieve small, even stitches, while other cultures use larger, more random ones. (see also utility quilting)

**raw edge** The cut, unfinished edge of a piece of fabric.

**reverse appliqué** An appliqué technique in which the top layers of fabric are cut away to reveal the design underneath.

**rotary cutting** A method of cutting fabric that requires a special round-bladed cutter, a self-healing mat marked with a grid measurement, and a thick plastic ruler. Multiple layers of strips or shapes can be cut cleanly and accurately.

**sampler** A type of quilt in which each block is made from a different pattern. The idea is widely used by learning quilters who want to explore a variety of designs and for making group quilts.

**sashiko** A type of Japanese quilting used to hold several layers of fabric together. The patterns are generally blue and white in geometric designs.

**sashing** Strips of fabric placed between blocks to delineate or separate individual blocks.

**scale** The size of a pattern in relationship to other elements in a design.

**scrap** A fragment or remnant of fabric that can be used in patchwork or appliqué.

**secondary colors** The three colors that are created when two primary colors are combined. Red + yellow makes orange, yellow + blue makes green, and blue + red makes purple.

**secondary pattern** The overall design that sometimes results—often unexpectedly—when the blocks of a quilt are combined.

**Seminole patchwork** A strip-piecing technique developed by women in the Seminole tribe in Florida. Strips of fabric are combined in rows and then cut at various angles and restitched to make elaborate bands of pattern.

**set-in seam** A seam in which two pieces are joined at an angle into which a third piece must be inserted. A continuous seam is not possible, so the seams must be sewn in separate steps.

**setting blocks** Blocks—usually plain squares or triangles—used to separate or fill out areas between decorative blocks.

**setting pattern** Also called the set, this term describes the way in which blocks are arranged in a quilt. Most blocks are "set square" at right angles to the edges of the quilt, but many quilts have the blocks turned "on point" with the edges of the blocks running diagonally across the quilt.

**shadow appliqué** An appliqué technique in which a sheer fabric is laid over the design and stitched in place to create a muted effect. Sometimes called shadow quilting.

**speed piecing** (see chain piecing)

**stained glass appliqué** An appliqué technique in which shapes are outlined with thin bias strips to create the effect of leaded stained glass designs.

**stencil** A pattern made from cardboard, plastic, metal, or wood that can be traced around to provide outlines for appliqué shapes or guidelines for quilting.

**stitch-and-flip** A patchwork technique in which shapes are stitched right sides together, then opened out for a new piece to be added. The method is often worked on a backing fabric for stability.

**strippy** A traditional quilt design in which vertical strips are combined across the width of the quilt and decorated with elaborate bands of quilting. The pattern is called "Bars" in the Amish community.

**stuffed quilting** (see trapunto)

**template** A pattern made from cardboard, plastic, metal, or wood used to mark patterns for patchwork or appliqué.

**tertiary colors** The colors that are created when a primary color is combined with a secondary color.

**trapunto** A quilting technique in which areas of the design are stuffed from behind to create a raised texture on the surface of the quilt.

**turned-edge appliqué** The most traditional appliqué technique, in which the raw edges of each appliqué shape are turned under with the point of the needle and sewn in place.

**tying** A traditional quilting technique in which a length of thread, yarn, or string is taken through all three layers of the quilt and tied, or knotted, on the surface. The knot can be worked on the front or the back of the quilt.

**utility quilting** A term encompassing several types of big-stitch quilting, in which the stitching can be accomplished more quickly than with fine hand quilting. Stitches tend to be larger and more randomly sized. Utility quilting is found on many African-American quilts, and includes sashiko and tying.

**value** A term used to describe the lightness or darkness of a color. A fabric's value can be greatly affected by the colors and values of the adjacent fabrics.

**wadding** (see batting)

**wholecloth** A quilt made from a single piece of fabric in which the quilting is the decoration. The fabric can be solid-colored or patterned, but the design uses no patchwork or appliqué.

# Index

# Acknowledgments

To David, always supportive and encouraging.

All finished quilts shown in the book are in the collection of the author except page 15, collection of Pat Thompson Patza, and page 20 (top) collection of Patricia Cox.

Thanks to Mark Hines, who photographed all the quilts except page 20 (top).

A special thank you to Pat Thompson Patza, who not only stitched the most projects—four—but also helped me assemble the finished quilts on page 60, and to Linda Benson of Fabric Fusion in Brown Deer, Wisconsin, who helped Pat design the Hawaiian appliqué cushion.

Thanks as well to The Cutting Table in Milwaukee, Wisconsin, for lending us the equipment used in the photographs.

The projects were stitched by
Tricia Glaister: Sashiko
Kathleen Golden: Log cabin
Karen Peck Katz: Rail fence, Nine-patch
Pat Thompson Patza: Hawaiian appliqué, Turned-edge appliqué, Bias strip appliqué, Hand quilting
Barbara Ritchey: Pictorial landscape, Machine appliqué
Joanne Sook: Curves, Basket
Patsy Tighe: English paper piecing, Broderie perse
Jane Walton: Four-patch (star), Reverse appliqué, Shadow appliqué

And of course, to all at Collins & Brown, especially Marie Clayton and Jane Ellis.